Exploring Essential Oils

Cole L. Woolley, PhD

EXPLORING ESSENTIAL OILS

Cover illustration and design by McKenna Woolley
Illustrations by McKenna Woolley
Graphics and photos by Philip Woolley
Molecule Structures by Cole L. Woolley, PhD
Book preparation by Gretchen Fuller (inktobook.com)

The uses of essential oils in this book are only suggestions. The reader is responsible for the choices made in using essential oils. The examples of essential oils in this book are based on the common species of essential oils used throughout the world. The author does not endorse any specific label or brand of essential oils. This book is only for educational purposes.

Edited by Jacqueline Woolley, Fred Woolley, Adrienne Woolley, and Eric Woolley

Published by Little Goat, LLC
Highland, Utah 84003
www.ExploringEO.com
ISBN: 978-0-692-93572-9
First Edition: August 2017
Printed in the United States of America

Table of Contents

Introduction

What You Need to Know about Essential Oils

"Mom, where do essential oils come from?"

You have probably heard something like this before. You may have asked a similar question. When you hear these curious questions, are you prepared with an answer?

"Mommy, are essential oils like the motor oil Daddy puts in the cars?"

"How does lavender oil get from the field and into the bottle?"

"How can a whole plant fit into a tiny seed?"

I like listening to the curious questions of innocent children because they want to learn about the big, new world around them. They are not afraid to ask questions. I find that most adults have similar questions but are sometimes afraid to ask them. As an adult you do not want to make mistakes, yet you need **confidence**. You want to sound intelligent and educated. You want to have the answers to questions about essential oils. You need confidence in explaining essential oils to your family, friends, and strangers.

The purpose of this book is to explore such questions and to provide you with the best and easiest answers for yourself and your friends. The answers to simple questions in this book will provide vocabulary and phrases you can share. The topics of this book will help you intelligently speak about essential oils. I have found that the best way for you to learn about essential oils is to teach and inform others around you. Look for **Dr. Woolley's Challenges** to help you gain confidence sharing your essential oil experiences.

This book is not intended to be read like a novel; from first to last chapter. Feel free to skip to the topics that you need most. There are a few technical chapters. Just skim over them or skip them and then return to them later. Highlight the phrases and words that you want to memorize. Use words and phrases from this book to describe your essential oil experiences.

You may meet people who will ask you simple and technical questions about essential oils. You may be asked to train others about essential oils. You may be asked to give talks to small and large groups. This book will help you have confidence when the time comes for you to be a leader and a teacher.

1

Essential Oils Are

WHY ARE THEY "ESSENTIAL"?

I hear this question often and there are many acceptable ways to answer it. Here are three of my favorite scientific explanations.

First, they are essential for survival. Plants produce essential oils and use them to survive in their environments. They use them to defend their growing area. They use them to scare away insects and other predators that would eat their leaves. They use them to attract animals and insects to pollinate their flowers.

Second, they are the essence of plants. Essence is a word used to describe the aroma of a plant, flower, root, or fruit. Describing the essence creates a "word picture" of the essential oil aroma. For example, orange essential oil has the essence of "citrusy, orangey, fresh, clean, and sweet".

Third, they are essential for animals and humans. We use essential oils for our health. We use them for their attractive, natural fragrances. We use them to maintain our well-being and to stay healthy. We use them to lift our moods and stabilize our emotions.

WHY ARE THEY CALLED "OILS"?

As children, we learned that words and terms can look and sound similar but are very different in use, form, and function. When people hear the word "oil" several images may materialize in their brains. They may envision motor oil, cooking oil, olive oil, or massage oil. When people hear the two words "essential oil" used together for the first time, they may have difficulty picturing a concept in their heads. Before I explore what an essential oil is, I need to discuss what it is not.

Essential oils are not greasy. Many of the oils we are accustomed to can be described as greasy or slippery. Essential oils are neither greasy, nor slippery. Certain oils are meant for cooking, like vegetable oil or olive oil. Essential oils, however, are not cooking oils. Other oils are refined and designed for lubrication like motor oil or lubrication oil. Essential oils are not lubricating oils. Now let's find out why essential oils are called "oils".

First, we call it an "oil" because it floats on water. Simple, right? Oil does not mix in water. When you combine oil and water, you will see two distinct and separate liquid layers.

Try this simple experiment at home. Fill a clear jar a quarter-full with tap water. Add vegetable oil until you can see a layer form on top. Immediately you will see that the vegetable oil floats on top of the water. Secure a lid to the jar and shake vigorously. What happens? Within seconds, the vegetable oil forms tiny droplets throughout the water. Let it sit on the countertop for 1 minute while you watch. What happens now? The tiny oil droplets move to the top and join the oil layer. The water becomes clear and there are two liquid layers again. Most essential oils act the same; they float on top of water.

Second, we call it an "oil" because it is mostly composed of Carbon and Hydrogen atoms. Molecules containing mainly Carbon and Hydrogen atoms do NOT mix with water and are lighter (less dense) than water, so they float on water. Scientists refer to molecules that are composed of ONLY Hydrogen and Carbon atoms as **hydrocarbons.** Vegetable oils are mostly hydrocarbon in nature; that is why they float.

ESSENTIAL OIL DEFINITION LIST

You may feel uncertain or lack the confidence to share your essential oil experiences with your family, friends, and coworkers. As you use essential oils they will start asking questions. It is common to hear questions like, "What are essential oils?" "Where do essential oils come from?"

Here is a list of phrases and definitions that may help you describe essential oils to your family and friends. Some are very simple while others may be more technical. As you use the simple phrases, you will find yourself becoming more confident. Use them in your emails and in your social media posts. Use them in social conversations and in training sessions. Practice saying these phrases to yourself. This book will help you understand the world of essential oils.

1. Essential oils are produced by plants.
2. Essential oils are the aroma molecules of plants.
3. Essential oils help plants and trees survive.
4. Essential oils help plants defend their growing space.
5. Essential oils help plants attract pollinators.
6. Essential oils help plants to expand their growing domain.
7. Essential oils are aromatic liquids produced by special plant cells.
8. Essential oils are stored in the leaves, stems, fruit, or roots of plants.
9. Essential oils float on water.
10. Essential oils are natural remedies.
11. Essential oils are used by humans to promote health and well-being.
12. Essential oils are released from harvested plants by Steam Distillation.
13. Essential oils are expressed from citrus fruits by Cold-Pressing.
14. Essential oils are steam distilled from harvested plant biomass.

15. Essential oils are completely natural, not synthetic.
16. Essential oils may trigger emotional changes.
17. Essential oils are secondary products of photosynthesis.
18. Essential oils contain 100-300 different molecules.
19. Essential oils contain Monoterpene and Sesquiterpene molecules.
20. Essential oil molecules are mainly composed of Carbon and Hydrogen atoms.
21. Essential oils contain Oxygenated Monoterpene and Oxygenated Sesquiterpene molecules.
22. Essential oil composition is determined by plant DNA.
23. Essential oil composition is consistent within each plant species.
24. Essential oils are the intelligence of plants.
25. Essential oil molecules are used by plants to communicate.
26. Essential oils may be applied to the skin.
27. Essential oils may be ingested or added to food
28. Essential oils may be inhaled into the lungs and sinuses.
29. Essential oil aromas are detected by olfactory nerves in the nose.
30. Essential oil molecules have unique aromas.
31. Essential oil aromas change as molecules evaporate from the skin.
32. Essential oil molecules exist in predictable percentages for each species.
33. Essential oils have been thoroughly studied by scientists.
34. Essential oils have been thoroughly documented in scientific literature.
35. Essential oils from different species contain different molecules.
36. Essential oils were anciently prepared by infusion into vegetable oils.
37. Essential oils were used as traditional medicines.

38. Essential oils were historically used in spiritual ceremonies.
39. Essential oils were used by ancient people for survival.

You may not understand all of these phrases now, but you will. Read this book and other books by Dr. Cole Woolley, PhD to achieve your goal of CONFIDENCE. Confidence starts one day at a time, one step at a time, one phrase at a time.

EXPLORING SUMMARY

- Plants use essential oils for their survival.
- Essential oils are the essence or aroma of a plant
- Essential oils are not greasy like cooking oils.
- Essential oils generally float on water and do not mix with water.
- Essential oils are mostly composed of Hydrogen and Carbon atoms.

GLOSSARY

Essential: Containing the essence or aroma of a plant; containing the vital components.

Oil: A substance that floats on water.

Essential oil: The aromatic molecules produced by plants, bushes, and trees.

Hydrocarbon: Molecules containing only Hydrogen and Carbon atoms.

DR. WOOLLEY'S CHALLENGE

- Choose and memorize 5 phrases from the essential oil definitions list.
- Use 3 of the essential oil definitions in emails, social media, and conversations this week.
- Tell a child or adult about essential oils using 3 of your memorized definitions.

2

Plants Grow

In the spring, plants and trees sprout leaves and branches. A peppermint plant can grow to 2 feet (70 cm) in 60 days. A corn stalk can grow 6 feet (2 meters) tall, while a pole bean plant can grow up to 8 feet (2.5 meters) in the same amount of time. How is it done? On a molecular level, how do plants grow? How do they know how to grow leaves, flowers, and fruits? How do they produce essential oil molecules? Are plants smart? In this chapter, we will explore these common questions regarding the rapid growth of plants.

INPUTS FOR PLANT GROWTH

Living plants require nourishment to grow. Take away even one of the vital nutrients and you will see stunted plant growth and eventual death. These vital plant nutrients are invisible to your eyes.

For humans to grow, they need vitamins and minerals, Oxygen to breathe, water to drink, and food to eat. In the long-run, humans also need shelter, warmth, and belonging. Food provides humans the carbohydrate, protein, and fat nutrients as necessary building blocks for growth. Taking away any one of these nutrient inputs can stunt the growth of a child.

Plants also depend on several unique nutrients or inputs in order to grow. You have observed plant growth each spring and summer with new branches, new leaves, new flowers, and new fruit.

One important reason that plants do not grow in cold winter months is that water is frozen in the ground and within the plant. Plants use water to transport nutrients from the leaves to the roots and then back again. Frozen water means no movement of nutrients.

Here are some important nutrient inputs for plant growth:

1. Warmth
2. Sunlight
3. Carbon Dioxide from the air
4. Water from the ground and air
5. Minerals from the ground

Warmth Input. A plant's growth requires water to be in liquid form. In the winter months when temperatures fall below the freezing point 32°F (0°C), plants are generally dormant (no growth). Plants require liquid water to flow through their "plant-type circulatory system" in order to grow. Even when soil temperatures in the spring are between 33-50°F (1-10°C), liquid water is often scarce and slow moving. However, when the soil temperature exceeds 52°F (11°C) and soil water is available, then plants start moving vital liquid water from roots to leaves.

Sunlight Input. Sunlight provides energy for plants to grow. Plants capture the sun's energy in their leaves. In plants this radiation energy from the sun is converted into **ATP biochemical energy molecules**. The ATP biochemical energy molecule promotes growth in roots, stems, leaves, flowers, and fruit.

Since daylight hours are longest during the summer months, plants receive more ATP biochemical energy molecules than during the shorter winter months. Essential oils are produced during the summer months with the aid of sunlight and ATP biochemical energy molecules.

Carbon Dioxide Input. Not Oxygen? Yes, unlike the human and animal need for Oxygen to breathe, plants need Carbon Dioxide for growth. This is the same Carbon Dioxide gas that humans and animals exhale as a waste product of respiration. Carbon Dioxide gas enters plants through small openings called **stomata** located on the leaf surface. Carbon Dioxide (CO_2) gas molecules contain one atom of Carbon and two (di-) atoms of Oxygen (-oxide).

Plants need the Carbon atoms as building blocks for large, structural growth molecules. Plants connect Carbon atoms into long chains that can contain hundreds and thousands of connected Carbon atoms. Essential oil molecules are also produced by linking Carbon atoms together.

Plants do not need the abundant Oxygen atoms from Carbon Dioxide molecules. Therefore, plants "exhale" Oxygen gas through the stomata openings into the surrounding air. Oxygen (O_2) gas molecules are composed of two Oxygen atoms. Insects, mammals, and humans depend on this Oxygen gas for survival. In conjunction, plants depend on Carbon Dioxide gas exhaled from humans and animals. Humans depend on plants and plants depend on humans.

Water Input. Water is like the circulatory blood of plants. In plants, water flows up through small tubes called **xylem** (pronounced Z-EYE-lum) to transport minerals from the soil to the leaves. Sugars produced in the leaves are transported throughout the plant using other small tubes called **phloem** (pronounced FLOW-em).

Water (H_2O) is composed of two Hydrogen atoms connected to one Oxygen atom. Plants use the Hydrogen atoms from water to connect to Carbon atoms from Carbon Dioxide to create simple and complex sugars. These sugars are converted into a variety of plant structures, including essential oils.

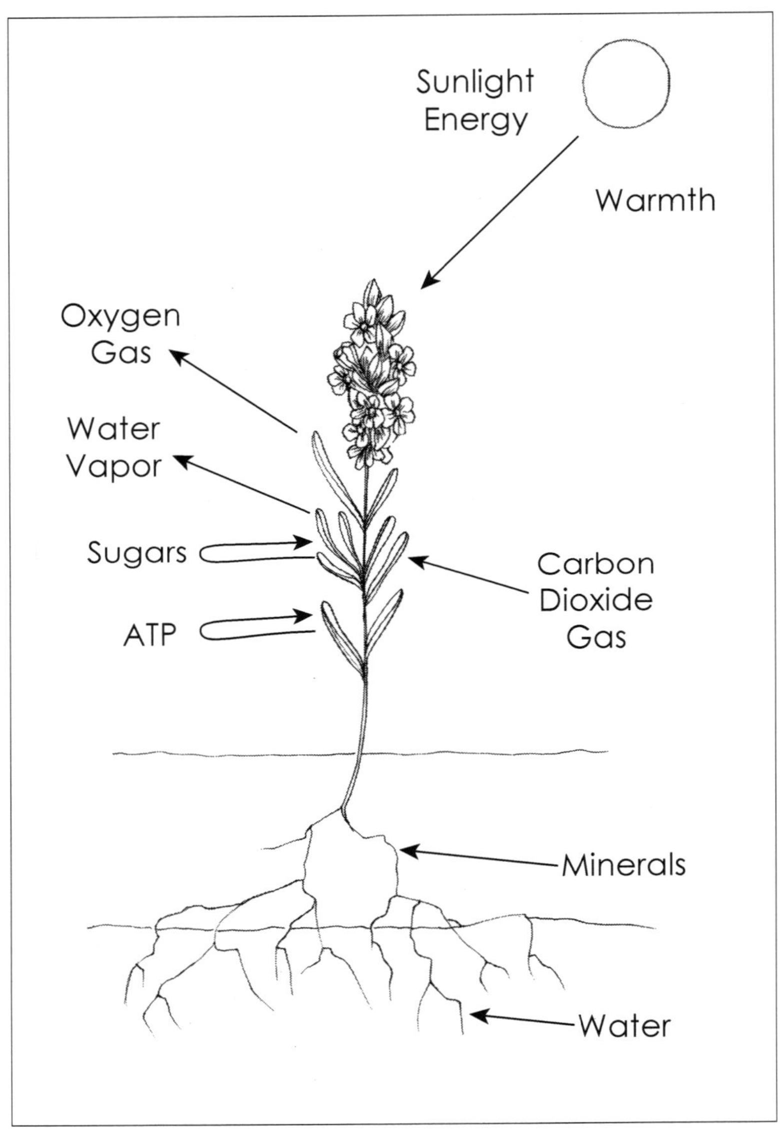

Figure 1. Inputs and outputs of plant photosynthesis.

Mineral Input. Minerals are essential to healthy, growing plants. The minerals and nutrients needed in highest abundance are Nitrogen, Phosphorus, and Potassium, which are common in commercial and natural fertilizers. The biochemical processes within each cell that convert Carbon Dioxide and water into sugars requires minerals. These minerals work as a team with ATP biochemical energy molecules to convert small molecules into larger molecules. Minerals help convert Carbon Dioxide and water into essential oil molecules.

OUTPUTS OF PLANT GROWTH

Plants provide humans and animals with key survival nutrients. Every human must have a minimum number of living plants and trees to survive. This co-existence is vital for both plants and humans. Plants give off or produce several important products:

1. Oxygen gas
2. Water vapor
3. ATP biochemical energy molecule
4. Sugars and Carbohydrates

Oxygen Gas Output. Plants give off Oxygen gas as a waste product of photosynthesis. Plants give off excess Oxygen gas through the small stomata openings in their leaves and stems. Human biochemistry requires Oxygen gas molecules from the air. Humans use Oxygen gas absorbed into the blood to convert digested food into ATP biochemical energy molecules. Humans transport Oxygen gas through the blood to every cell of the body in order to produce billions of ATP biochemical energy molecules every day.

Water Vapor Output. Plants release water vapor from their leaves in order to siphon water up from the soil (acts just like a soda straw). Plants release water vapor through the stomata openings in their leaves. This process is called **transpiration**. Most of the water vapor is simply from the circulating water that rises from the roots to the leaves. The release of water vapor increases the humidity surrounding the plant. Some of the water vapor condenses into liquid droplets during the cool night temperatures to restore water to the soil.

ATP Biochemical Energy Molecule Output. The leaves of a plant capture sunlight and convert it into ATP biochemical energy molecules. This ATP molecule is the energy currency used to operate all biochemical mechanisms within the plant. It takes numerous ATP molecules to connect Carbon, Hydrogen and Oxygen atoms to form sugar molecules and essential oil molecules. It takes hundreds of ATP biochemical energy molecules to convert Carbon Dioxide and water into one essential oil molecule.

Sugar and Carbohydrate Molecule Output. Plant biochemistry has a single purpose – transform Carbon Dioxide gas and liquid water into sugars using ATP molecules as the biochemical energy source. This process is known as **photosynthesis**. Plants connect six Carbon atoms and add a number of Hydrogen and Oxygen atoms to produce **sugar** molecules. The formation of sugars within plants is referred to as the **Primary Metabolism** pathway.

These sugar molecules are the biochemical building blocks for growth in all plants. When the plant connects thousands of sugar molecules, they create **carbohydrate** molecules. Complex, large carbohydrate molecules add structure to the plant for growth, like the wood of a tree or a growing flower. The structures of leaves, flowers, fruits, and seeds all start with the simple sugars photosynthesized from Carbon Dioxide and water.

In plants these sugar molecules can also be converted into essential oil molecules. Because essential oil molecules are converted from sugar molecules, the process is often referred to as

Figure 2. Plants require abundant ATP molecules to produce sugar molecules and essential oil molecules.

the **Secondary Metabolism** pathway. The conversion of essential oil molecules requires energy provided by numerous ATP biochemical energy molecules. Each species of aromatic plants produce 100-300 different molecules in their essential oil.

HUMANS DEPEND ON PLANTS

Humans use food for growth and health. Digested food is converted into billions of ATP biochemical energy molecules in the body. Digested food is also converted into sugar molecules. For humans the digested food produces all the building blocks needed for growth. There are three types of human foods: carbohydrates (containing Carbon, Hydrogen, and Oxygen atoms), proteins (containing Carbon, Hydrogen, Oxygen and Nitrogen atoms), and fats (containing Carbon, Hydrogen, and Oxygen atoms).

Most carbohydrate foods come from domesticated plant crops: carrots, potatoes, lettuce, rice, peaches, mangoes, etc. Most of the protein and fat nutrients necessary for humans comes in the form of animal meat, legumes, and grain. Farm animals get most of their food nutrients from plant life. Therefore, humans are both directly and indirectly dependent on plants for life, health, and survival.

EXPLORING SUMMARY

- Plants require warmth, sunlight, Carbon Dioxide gas, liquid water and minerals in order to carry out photosynthesis and grow.
- Plants must release Oxygen gas and water vapor in order to produce sugars by photosynthesis.
- Plant sugars are the building blocks for plant growth and constructing essential oil molecules.

GLOSSARY

Xylem (Z-EYE-lum): Vertically elongated plant cells that transport water and minerals up from the roots to the leaves.

Phloem (FLOW-em): Vertically plant cells connected like passenger cars on a commuter train that transport photosynthesized sugars up and down from the leaves to all parts of the plant.

Transpiration: The process of powering water transportation (from the roots, up through the hollow, narrow xylem cells, to the cells of the leaves and stems) by evaporation of water through the leaves' stomata openings.

Photosynthesis: The process plants use to capture sunlight energy and convert it to the ATP biochemical energy molecule. This process is also known as Primary Metabolism.

Biochemical energy: Plants, humans, and animals use the same ATP molecule as a source of energy to operate the biochemical functions to stay healthy and alive.

ATP: Adenosine TriPhosphate. This is the energy molecule used by plants and animals for growth, change, recovery, and activity.

Stomata: Small openings in leaves that allow Carbon Dioxide gas to enter. Stomata also provide for the escape of Oxygen gas and water vapor into the air.

Sugars: A variety of 5- or 6-Carbon molecules also containing numerous Hydrogen and Oxygen atoms. They are produced from Carbon Dioxide gas and water in the leaves of plants by photosynthesis.

Carbohydrate: A chain of connected sugar molecules composed of Carbon, Hydrogen, and Oxygen atoms.

Primary Metabolism: The process of converting sugar molecules into more complex carbohydrate molecules.

Secondary Metabolism: The process in plants that converts sugar molecules into essential oil molecules.

DR. WOOLLEY'S CHALLENGE

- Draw a diagram showing how plants grow using 5 inputs (warmth, sunlight, Carbon Dioxide, water, and minerals) and 4 outputs (Oxygen gas, water vapor, ATP, and sugars).
- Recite out loud the 5 inputs and 4 outputs of plant growth.
- Draw a diagram showing the origins of essential oil molecules in plants. Use the words sunlight, Carbon Dioxide, water, leaf, stem, ATP, sugar molecules and essential oil molecules.
- Explain to a child or adult how essential oil molecules originate from Carbon Dioxide and water.

3

Plants Produce and Store Essential Oils

Suppose you have a 10-year old daughter who wants to conduct a science project on essential oils. She decides to use citrus fruit (oranges, lemons, and grapefruits) for her experiments. "Mom, when I rub my hand on a lemon, I can't smell it like I can when I touch a peppermint leaf. How can I get the aroma out of the citrus fruits?"

The answer is to talk to your daughter about zesting the citrus rind or squeezing the pulp to release the essential oil. Then she may ask, "Mom, how does the fruit produce the essential oil?" You let her know that plants produce essential oil molecules from Carbon Dioxide molecules in the air and water molecules in the soil.

EXODERMAL AND ENDODERMAL SOURCES OF ESSENTIAL OILS

You may have noticed that many essential oils can be released from plants simply by touching them. Touching lavender, peppermint, sage, or thyme plants results in essential oil molecules attached to your hand. These are examples of exodermal (meaning "exterior of the skin") cell production of essential oils on plants, shrubs, and trees. There are also an abundance of plants and trees that produce and store their essential oils in the endodermal (meaning "within the skin") cells that are not released when they are touched. Some examples include tree wood, citrus fruits, and plant roots. These exodermal and endodermal secretory (meaning "that secrete or produce") cells produce and store essential oil molecules.

EXODERMAL SECRETORY CELLS

When you touch lavender, peppermint, thyme, or spearmint leaves, some of the essential oil is transferred to your hands. These are examples of plants that produce and store their essential oil on the exterior of the plant in exodermal cells. Exodermal cells that produce and store essential oils look like hair or fur on the cellular surface of leaves and stems. These protrusions are known as **trichomes** (pronounced TRY-combs).

Many flowering herbs, leafy plants, and grasses produce exodermal trichomes. They include lavender, sage, rosemary, peppermint, hyssop, marjoram, clary sage, melissa, oregano, spearmint, yarrow, lemon myrtle, patchouli, geranium, tea tree, petitgrain, and lemongrass. There are also several flowers in this exodermal category including ylang ylang, German chamomile, Roman chamomile, helichrysum, clove, neroli, and rose. Touching these plants and flowers will transfer some essential oil molecules from their delicate trichomes onto your fingers.

Trichomes Help Plants Communicate. Plants produce and store essential oil molecules in exodermal trichomes in order to communicate with their environment. One of the major purposes is to transmit messages like "REPEL" or "ATTRACT". Trichomes release essential oil molecules to communicate with the world that surrounds them. Unlike humans and animals that use sounds, words, or gestures; plants communicate using essential oil molecules.

A plant's greatest defense to avoid being eaten is to produce, store, and release essential oil molecules. Hungry **herbivores** like grasshoppers, deer, and mice can be repelled by essential oil molecules. Some essential oil molecules are distasteful to herbivores. They deliver a warning message to the herbivore such as, "Hey, get away from me!" or "You do not want to nibble on me or else!" Since plants and trees are rooted to the ground, they cannot run away from potential danger. They must rely on essential oil molecules that move in the air and stick on passing animals. This is how trichomes play a vital role in a plant's survival.

In contrast, some plants communicate more friendly messages with their essential oil molecules. A plant uses its colorful flowers to attract visiting **pollinators** like bees, butterflies, birds, and mammals. These pollinators deliver pollen attached to their bodies to assist in pollinating fruits with viable seeds. Therefore, one way to promote the pollination process is to produce, store, and release essential oil molecules to attract pollinators. In this case the aromatic molecules in essential oils are used to make a plant seem desirable and tasty. These molecules deliver an enticing message to the pollinators like, "Stop and take a closer look" or "Yum! Try tasting my nectar."

Hair-like Trichomes. These exodermal secretory cells that produce and store essential oils have very fine hair-like structures. On some plants, they look like "peach fuzz" which is why they are called "hair" or "hair-like".

The Hair-like trichomes produce a significant percentage of the total plant essential oil, and their function is critical to plant survival. Approximately 30-80% of some plant's essential oil reserves are stored in Hair-like trichomes. Hair-like trichomes range in length from 50 – 1000 **micrometers** and in diameter from 20-100 micrometers. Human hair grows about 10 micrometers each day. A human hair is about 50 micrometers in diameter. This is where the description of Hair-like trichomes originates.

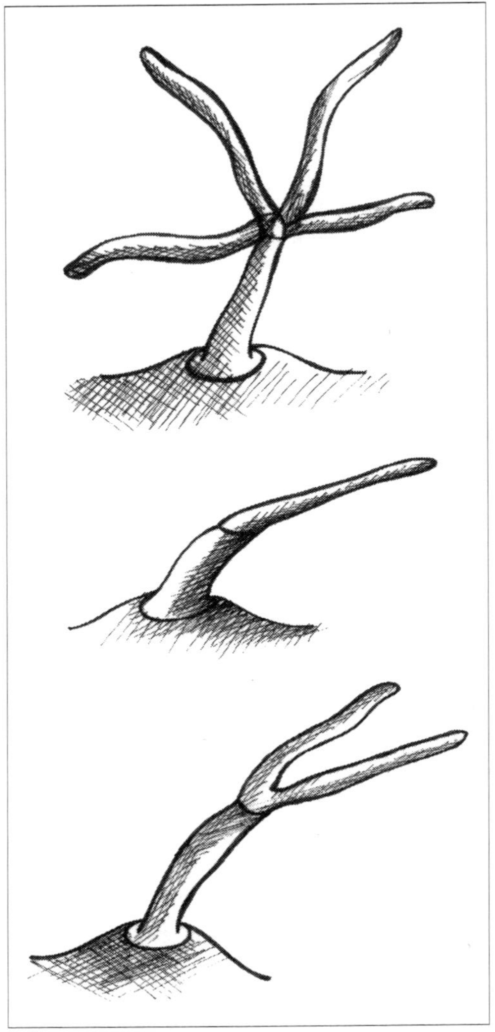

Figure 3. Various forms of Hair-like trichomes that produce and store essential oil molecules.

If you were to examine a lavender leaf under a microscope you would see a jungle of Hair-like trichomes covering the surface. Due to the delicate, flimsy nature of these Hair-like structures, it does not take much pressure to move them. The slightest movement releases a small cloud of essential oil molecules into the surrounding air. A butterfly walking on the surface, the passing touch of a deer, or the moving force of a breeze can cause the Hair-like trichomes to release essential oil molecules.

Aromatic plants that cover their surfaces with Hair-like trichomes have a great strategy for survival. When plants release the essential oil molecules from the Hair-like trichomes, this acts like sending an aromatic cloud of messages. They use these fine trichomes as their first warning and defense against being eaten. This is similar to a man with hairy arms that seemingly never gets bitten by mosquitos or flies because his sensitive hair warns of their presence. Insects are likely to be repelled just by crawling on these essential oil-releasing plant hairs. With insects being the largest consumer of plant matter on Earth, it makes sense that plants have ways of defending themselves from voracious herbivores like grasshoppers and caterpillars.

While some plants use Hair-like trichomes as a defensive strategy, others use them to attract visiting animals and insects using their essential oil aroma. Consider cats seeking out and rolling in catnip or humans gathering lavender leaves to make tea. We tend to keep plants we like and spread them around for our own use. For the plant, this means survival and thriving in broader domains.

Peltate (Glandular) Trichomes. Peltate (meaning "shield-like") trichomes are another type of exodermal cells that produce and store essential oil molecules in plants. I sometimes refer to them as "globular trichomes" due to their globe-like shape. These surface cells start out looking like deflated balloons, but gradually expand as spherical globes as the plant matures. It takes herbivores more effort to release the essential oils stored in Peltate trichomes.

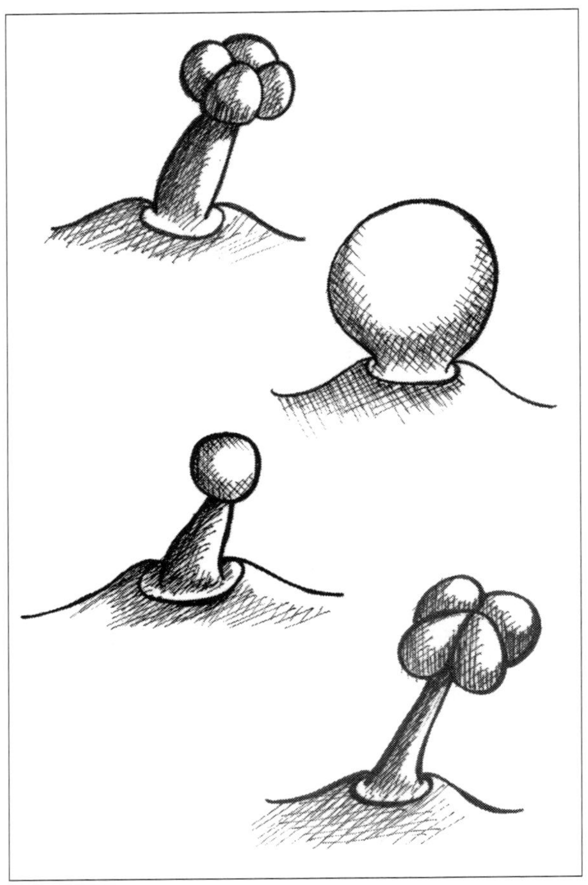

Figure 4. Variety of Peltate trichomes that produce and store essential oil molecules.

The release of essential oils from Peltate trichomes sends out a larger aromatic cloud of messages to the environment. This cloud is considerably larger than the one released by Hair-like trichomes. It is as if the plant is "shouting" or "proclaiming" its biochemical message of "STAY AWAY!"

Animals Detect Essential Oil Molecules from Trichomes. Herbivores interacting with plants can readily interpret aromatic signals. Humans and animals detect the aroma of aromatic molecules using olfactory receptors and olfactory nerves in their nasal cavities. Inhaling the molecules gives the olfactory nerve endings a chance to detect and identify the essential oil molecules.

Humans possess a moderate sense of smell. Elephants and bears have 4 times the human sense of smell. Rats, opossums, cows, turtles, mice, and horses enjoy 3 times the human sense of smell. Frogs, dogs, rabbits, and guinea pigs possess a sense of smell that is just 2 times that of humans. All of them use their keen sense of smell to choose the plants they want to consume. The olfactory nerves of herbivores is directly responsible for their selection of foods.

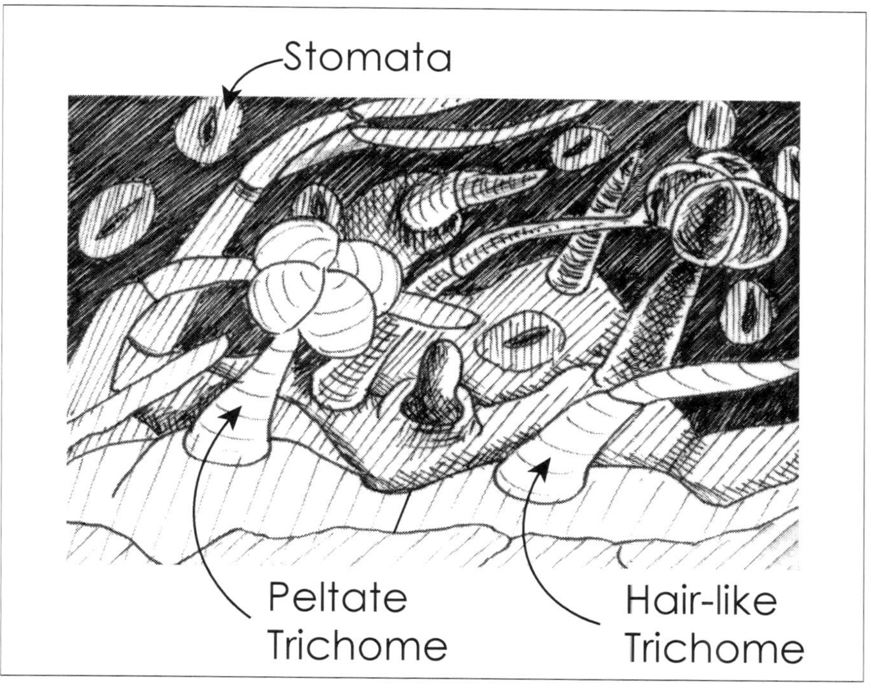

Figure 5. Combination of Hair-like and Peltate trichomes produce and store essential oil molecules.

Insects detect and "read" the molecules of essential oil with their long antennae mounted atop their heads. Nerve receptors located on the tip of the antennae detect the essential oil molecules. Once detected, a neural response corresponding to the molecule is sent to the brain. The brain decodes the neural signal based on the structures of the essential oil molecules. Most insects have a keen sense of smell. Insects like ants, bees, wasps, beetles, flies, dragonflies, mosquitos, butterflies, moths, and grasshoppers detect and decipher the signals of essential oil molecules so they know what plants to eat and what plants to avoid.

ENDODERMAL SECRETORY CELLS

You may be surprised how many essential oils are produced and stored within the interior of plants, trees, roots, and fruit. You may have smelled the zested essential oils from within a lemon peel or detected the piney aroma of freshly cut evergreen trees. In addition, there are fresh ginger roots and dried cinnamon bark sticks that you find at the grocery store that give off strong aromas when peeled or crushed. All of these plants produce and store essential oils within their bark, plant, wood, or fruit peel.

Citrus Fruit Peel. Citrus fruits produce and store essential oils in spherical sacs located just below the surface of the peel. These fruits include oranges, lemons, limes, grapefruits, tangerines, mandarins, and many other citrus varieties. Essential oil molecules are produced and stored in these secretory sacs. The secretory sacs start out like deflated balloons, but fill up with essential oil as the fruit ripens. Citrus oils are expressed from citrus peels by industrial Cold-Press processes.

Roots. Some plants like valerian, ginger, and vetiver produce and store their essential oils in roots instead of the fruit, leaf or stem. The essential oils are produced and stored in spherical secretory sacs. The upper, green part of these plants are typically not aromatic. Once the above-ground plant dies off, the roots are harvested, chopped up, and steam distilled.

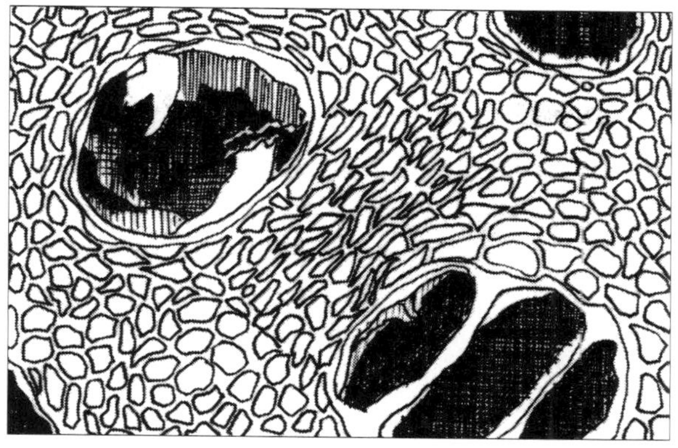

Figure 6. Secretory sacs that produce and store essential oil molecules in an orange peel.

Seeds. Some essential oils are distilled from plant seeds and kernels. Many plants produce and store essential oil within the seed kernel including carrot, cardamom, nutmeg, fennel, dill, coriander, cumin, and anise. The seeds are harvested, dried, and steam distilled to release the essential oil.

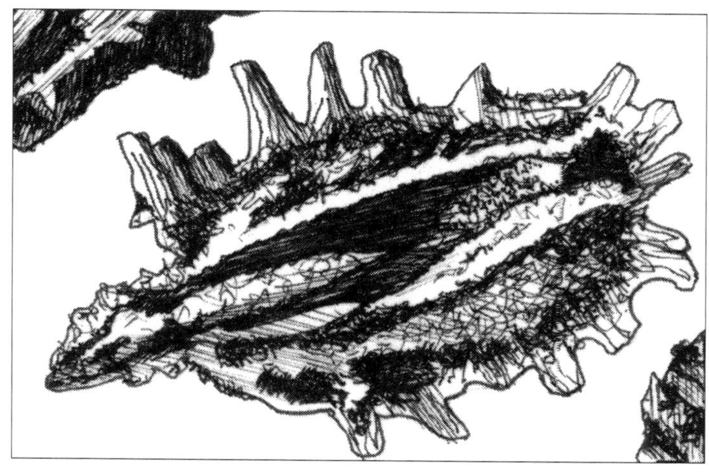

Figure 7. Carrot seeds produce and store essential oil molecules.

Bark. Some very unique trees and woody plants produce essential oil in their bark, including cinnamon and cassia. The inner wood is not aromatic, just the bark. Cinnamon leaf and cassia leaf also contain essential oil molecules, but are significantly different from the essential oil of the bark. Many of these trees are grown on plantations and **coppiced** (cut at the ground level) each 12-18 months to harvest the 2 inch (5 cm) diameter sprouts. The bark is stripped off the sprouts, allowed to dry, and typically cut to lengths for the spice industry. The atypical pieces are collected for Steam Distillation to release the essential oil molecules.

Oleogum-resin. Some trees produce oleogum-resin when the bark or inner bark is wounded. You may have experienced oleogum-resin on pine, fir, or spruce trees. The historical trade of oleogum-resins harvested from frankincense, galbanum, elemi, copal, and myrrh trees is important to the essential oil industry. Many of these latter trees have been tapped for over 5000 years by locals in Oman, Yemen, Somalia, Ethiopia, India, Central America, South America, and the Philippines. They are tapped once a year during the hottest season in order for the tree to produce the most oleogum-resin. After the harvest, the oleogum-resin forms a scab that seals the bark. These trees heal the small wound within 12 months and stay healthy for centuries.

Flower Petals. Flowers of many plants contain essential oil molecules. Some flower petals like ylang ylang, rose, clove bud, and neroli are steam distilled to produce wonderfully aromatic essential oils. Other flowering heads are harvested with minimal harvesting of stems and leaves. This is the case with essential oils steam distilled from flowering German chamomile, Roman chamomile, helichrysum, and davana.

Needles. Most coniferous trees produce a distinct essential oil in their needle-shaped leaves. They produce secretory (glandular) sacs within the tissue of the needles. The needle essential oil is typically "piney" in aroma, but may also possess a "floral" smell.

Figure 8. Oleogum-resin exuding from frankincense tree in Oman.

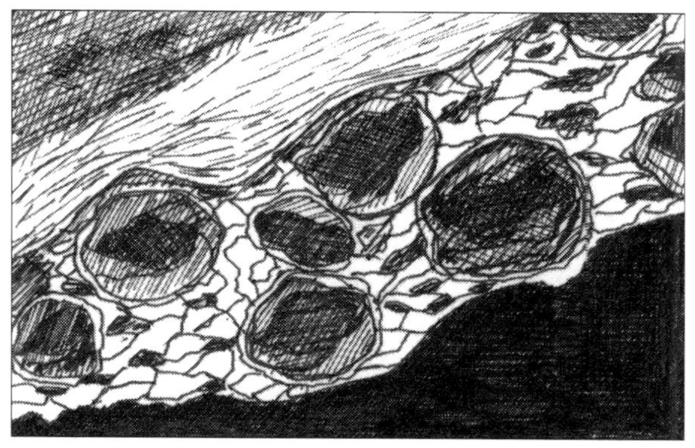

Figure 9. Secretory sacs produce and store essential oil molecules in clove buds.

Coniferous trees that produce aromatic needles include balsam fir, black spruce, blue spruce, Virginia cedarwood, pine, fir, cypress, Virginia juniper, Douglas fir, western red cedar and hundreds of other conifer species throughout the world. Try picking a needle from one of these trees and crushing the tissue to release the essential oil.

In some operations, coniferous branches are collected at logging sites where they are considered a waste product. In contrast, some needle-laden branches are selectively harvested from plantation-grown trees (e.g., black spruce and Virginia juniper). The branches are collected, chipped and steam distilled to release the essential oil molecules.

Tree Growth Rings. Many conifer trees and some unique trees contain essential oil molecules in their growth rings and heartwood. Their heartwood and growth rings contain essential oils that are more concentrated in high molecular weight molecules which possess a "woody" aroma. These include pine, fir, spruce, juniper, cedarwood, palo santo, sandalwood, western red cedar, Japanese *hinoki*, Taiwan red *hinoki*, and hundreds of other tree species.

Many of these trees are harvested from private and public lands by the lumber industry. At lumber-producing sawmills, the scrap lumber, bark, and sawdust are collected and chipped into small pieces for Steam Distillation. Sustainable sandalwood is grown on plantations in Australia where they are harvested 15-20 years after planting. Some trees, including Texas cedarwood and western juniper, are harvested to clear land for farmers and ranchers. Conifer trees that were planted for the Christmas tree market but have already passed their prime harvesting years are often harvested and chipped for Steam Distillation. There are many examples of cultivated and wild-crafted trees that supply a renewable source of essential oils.

EXPLORING SUMMARY

- Insects, birds and land animals use olfactory nerve endings to detect and identify essential oil molecules in plants.
- Plants produce and store essential oils within leaves, flowers, stems, fruits, seeds, needles, growth rings, and roots.
- Special exodermal cells called Hair-like trichomes and Peltate (glandular) trichomes produce and store essential oils on the plant surface.
- Many plants produce essential oils within special endodermal cells called secretory sacs.
- Citrus essential oils are produced and stored in endodermal spherical sacs embedded in the peel of citrus fruits.
- Many conifer and frankincense trees produce oleogum-resin when a tree is wounded.

GLOSSARY

Exodermal: Describing secretory cells that form on the outer surface of plants and trees.

Endodermal: Describing secretory cells that grow within plants and trees.

Secretory: Describing plant cells that produce or secrete essential oil molecules.

Trichome (TRY-comb): Exodermal plant cells that produce and store essential oil molecules.

Hair-like Trichome: Exodermal trichome cells that look like fine hair that produce and store essential oil molecules.

Micrometer: A unit of length for very small objects that are difficult to see with the human eyes.

Peltate (Glandular) Trichome: Exodermal trichome cells that are spherical in shape that produce and store essential oil molecules.

Secretory Sacs: Endodermal spherical cells or groups of cells that produce and store essential oils within plant fruit, roots, stems, leaves, and seeds.

Coppice (KAW-pes): The practice of routinely harvesting young sprouts from tree stumps.

Oleogum-resin: The sticky sap that flows from tree wounds that contains essential oil, water-soluble gum, and resin molecules.

Herbivore: Insects and animals that only eat plants and herbs.

Pollinator: Any insect or animal that assists in transferring pollen grains from one plant to another.

DR. WOOLLEY'S CHALLENGE

- Draw a rough sketch of 5 Hair-like trichomes surrounding 1 Peltate (glandular) trichome.
- Explain to a child or an adult the different ways that plants store essential oils (e.g., trichomes on peppermint, secretory sacs in citrus fruit peel, growth rings on trees, and glandular sacs in conifer needles).

4

Plants Use Essential Oils

Have you ever considered how plants use the essential oil molecules? Have you ever thought that plants need essential oils to survive? I've introduced some of their uses in the last chapter.

"What does a lavender plant do with the essential oil molecules it produces?"

"What happens to the essential oil molecules during cold, snowy winters?"

"What is the purpose of producing essential oil molecules in the orange fruit peel?"

"Why does a pine tree produce sticky sap from a broken branch?"

You may have a chance to answer similar questions from your children, grandchildren, or friends. It is a good idea to be confidently prepared with a few answers.

PRESERVING THEIR DOMAIN

Aromatic plants, shrubs, and trees produce and use essential oil molecules to preserve their domain (space) above and below the ground. They do this to preserve the necessary resources around them in order to survive and thrive. Plants need space below ground to spread out their root network and to anchor themselves. This is called their **soil domain.** Their complex root system absorbs ground water and soil minerals during the growing season.

Plants require space above ground to pull in Carbon Dioxide gas from the air in order to generate great quantities of ATP biochemical energy molecules. In turn, they also need to produce sugars and carbohydrates to grow new leaves, new branches, extend their roots, and produce essential oil molecules. This is called their **air domain.** Plants also need this air space to transpire excess water vapor and release excess Oxygen gas.

Plants produce essential oil molecules to preserve their soil domain and their air domain. Letting another plant or tree crowd into their domain could put their survival at risk. Just as humans need and defend their personal space and living space, plants have similar needs. An excellent way they can preserve their soil domain and air domain is with essential oil molecules.

Inhibiting Seed Germination. Plants and trees require soil domain and air domain to survive. Some trees use essential oil molecules to guard their domain. Conifer trees like pine, fir, and spruce species produce essential oil molecules in their needles (leaves). They produce these essential oil molecules for two major purposes – to make their needles distasteful to animals and insects; and to inhibit seed germination within their soil domain.

In a forest setting where the conifer trees are not disturbed, you will likely see a thick blanket of fallen, brown needles covering the ground under the tree. This marks the topsoil domain of the conifer tree. This bed of needles causes high soil acidity, which inhibits seed germination. In addition, the essential oil molecules in the fallen needles discourage the germination of seeds. This includes inhibiting seed germination from neighboring plant

Figure 10. Evergreen tree showing branches (air domain) and roots (soil domain).

species and from the parent tree. The result is a bed of fallen conifer needles that maintains and creates a topsoil zone that protects the soil domain for the tree's massive root system.

Repelling Herbivores. Another purpose for essential oil molecules in conifer needles is to repel herbivores. Newly sprouted leaves are soft and very edible to animals and humans. However, as the conifer needles mature, the essential oil content increases. Common land-based herbivores like deer, elk, and moose will shy away from consuming mature conifer leaves due to the essential oil content. Only starvation during deep winter snows will force them to graze on pine and spruce needles.

To maintain air domain a conifer tree must be able to repel herbivores. The green, chlorophyll-containing needles that convert sunlight energy into ATP biochemical energy molecules need to be protected. Therefore, conifer trees produce essential oil molecules in their needles to deter herbivores. It's all about survival.

Attracting Pollinators

Some plants produce essential oils to get the attention of nectar-loving insects, birds, and land animals. Plants and animals have a co-dependent relationship – they need each other. Plants need to attract pollinators to produce viable seeds. Insects and birds recognize flowers by their shape, color patterns, and aroma in order to obtain sugary nectar. Each visit to feed on nectar results in pollen grains transferred from other flowers. This leads to cross pollination – a means of sharing genetic information with neighboring same-species plants and producing viable seeds.

Plants need pollinators to share their genetic information to strengthen their species. Pollinating insects and birds are very effective at inadvertently carrying neighboring plant genetic information found in pollen grains. This is truly a give-and-take relationship. The plants give up some biochemical energy to attract the pollinators and in return take an exchange of genetic information from neighboring same-species plants.

ATTRACTING SEED DISPERSERS

Many plants and trees produce tasty, essential oil-infused, fruit coatings around their seeds to attract animals. In the process of consuming the tasty fruit, they also consume the seeds. The seed remains undigested during the wandering travels of the animal. Eventually the intact, viable seeds are deposited some distance away from the original plant. Squirrels harvesting and caching pine cones in multiple locations is an excellent example of seed dispersal. One of the plant kingdom's greatest goals is to thrive and expand the range of growth for their species. Because animals are mobile, they meet the plant kingdom's requirement for seed dispersal.

Plants expend significant biochemical energy producing essential oil-laden flowers and fruit. Yet the spent biochemical energy is worth the results. Attracting fruit-eating birds and land animals accomplishes the plant's purpose for seed dispersal. These give-and-take relationships between plants and animals living in the same domain ensure survival for both, resulting in a win-win scenario.

The essential oils within citrus peels are used to send out signals to foraging insects and animals when the fruit is ripe. These signals to insects, birds, and large animals say, in aroma language: "Hey you, I'm sweet and juicy. Stop by and try me". Seed dispersal is the goal of every plant to expand their domain. They do this as a long-term strategy to preserve the species.

Expanding Geographic Domain. Using essential oil molecules to attract insects, birds, and mammals helps plants expand their **geographic domain.** A healthy spread of DNA between plants of the same species introduces strong attributes into future plant generations. Seeds that are spread by fruit-foraging animals help expand the number of plants in a wider geographic domain.

Citrus trees are always trying to expand their geographic domain. At the same time, grasses, flowers, bushes and other tree species are trying to expand into the same territory. This is like a war between plants. Sometimes the winner is the one that gets more seeds dispersed. Sometimes the winning species spreads into harsh climates where there is less competition.

Fir trees expand their geographic domain as glaciers recede due to climate change. At the same time, fields of grasses and flowers may lose geographic domain to expanding forests. This war to secure soil domain and air domain using essential oil molecules in flowers, fruit, and leaves is being waged every day and everywhere; maybe in your own backyard.

HEALING WOUNDS

One of the most common survival strategies of evergreen, conifer trees is to produce essential oil molecules in a mixture of essential oil, gum, and resin (oleogum-resin) to seal and heal wounds. Wind and weather damage can expose vital cells to potential damage. Such exposure can put the tree at further risk by damaging heat, bacteria, insects, and animals. Large animals can also damage conifers trees. Bears love to rub their backs on conifer trees. Deer and elk rub their velvet antlers on younger conifer trees. Woodpecker and flicker birds bore nesting holes into soft conifer trees. Humans cause damage when they trim branches or attempt to cut down trees. The only defense that these trees possess is to exude their sticky oleogum-resin to seal the wound and protect the tree.

The oleogum-resin within conifer trees is produced in **resin canals.** Cutting into or breaking a resin canal stimulates the production and flow of oleogum-resin. The oleogum-resin oozes out the resin canal and drips down to cover the open wound. The oleogum-resin will continue to flow until it hardens into a resin-like scab. This process is similar to when a scab is formed and hardens over a bleeding cut on your skin.

The frankincense trees of the Arabian and African deserts possess resin canals that secrete oleogum-resin. For 5000 years these trees

Figure 11. Oleogum-resin exuding from a broken pine branch.

Figure 12. Oleogum-resin exuding from a frankincense tree in Oman.

have been purposely wounded each year for their production of aromatic oleogum-resin. The most common frankincense oleogum-resin producing species include: *Boswellia sacra* in Oman and Yemen, *Boswellia carterii* in Somalia, *Boswellia frereana* in Somalia, *Boswellia papyrifera* in neighboring Ethiopia, and *Boswellia serrata* in India. After the harvest is completed, a fresh layer of oleogum-resin seals the wound to allow the frankincense tree to heal.

FIGHTING BACTERIAL AND FUNGAL DECAY

Pine species produce well-defined resin canals within the living mass of phloem cells just inside the bark. Making a wide, horizontal cut past the bark into the soft living phloem cells of the tree usually sever **axial** (vertical) **resin canals.** These axial resin canals surround the perimeter of the tree to protect it from major wounds. The oleogum-resin that exudes from axial resin canals seals the wound and forms a protective barrier against bacterial and fungal growth.

Figure 13. Cross-section of pine tree showing concentric growth rings and axial resin canals.

Unlike species of pine trees, there are NO resin canals found in the species of fir, hemlock, cedar, and juniper. The essential oil is locked up in each successive growth ring of the tree. When these trees are wounded, the high essential oil content in the growth rings protects the tree from invasion by bacteria, fungi, and insects.

Other conifer species like spruce, larch, cypress, and Douglas fir are the most prolific at producing oleogum-resin at wound sites. They typically possess a complex, connecting array of **radial** (horizontal) **resin canals.** Oleogum-resin quickly seals the wounds from weather-damage to protect against insects, bacteria, and fungi.

Fir trees possess a separate mechanism for defense. Fir trees possess **pitch blisters** situated on the exterior of their smooth bark. They look like bumps and are filled with sticky oleogum-resin. Pitch blisters can be found on alpine fir, noble fir, balsam fir, and Douglas fir trees. These pitch blisters hinder the invasion of burrowing insects and birds. The sticky oleogum-resin seals these wounds from further attack by insects and bacteria.

COMMUNICATING WITH THE ENVIRONMENT

Plants produce, store, and release essential oil molecules to communicate with their external environment. Since plants, bushes, and trees are rooted to the ground, they need some type of portable means of communication. Essential oil molecules act as the "words" they speak.

Communicating with Herbivores. Plants use essential oil molecules to communicate with wandering and migrating herbivores. Most herbivores have a greater sense of smell than vision. The essential oil molecules in aromatic plants is their greatest defense again foraging herbivores. I have watched mule deer pass by sage brush, pine trees, and spruce trees all winter long in the snow-covered mountains of Utah, sometimes resulting in death from starvation. Most insects avoid eating tomato plants due to their defensive essential oil content. Plants communicate with herbivores using essential oil molecules in order to survive.

Communicating with Plants. Scientists have discovered that plants communicate with each other using essential oil molecules. When insect or mammal herbivores begin feasting on aromatic plants, the plants respond by releasing essential oil molecules. The essential oil cloud moves outward to neighboring plants as a warning signal. Neighboring plants that detect the air-borne essential oil cloud begin to prepare their essential oil warning system. In this manner, plant communities can survive against potential threats by combining their defensive essential oil molecules.

EXPLORING SUMMARY

- Plants use essential oil molecules to protect and maintain their air domain and soil domain.
- Plants use essential oil molecules to repel herbivores (insects and animals).
- Plants use essential oils to attract pollinating insects and animals.
- Plants use essential oils to attract animals to feed on fruit for seed dispersal.
- Plants use essential oil molecules to expand the geographic range of their species.
- Plants use essential oil molecules to heal wounds caused by weather and animals.
- Plants use essential oils to protect against bacterial and fungal decay.
- Plants use essential oil molecules to communicate with foraging animals.
- Plants use essential oil molecules to communicate with their external environment.

GLOSSARY

Air Domain: The 3-dimensional space and resources in the air that a plant or tree occupies and uses.

Soil Domain: The 3-dimensional space and resources in the soil that a plant or tree occupies and uses.

Geographic Domain: The soil surface area where all plants or trees of a species grow (e.g., the two-needle pinyon pine tree grows throughout the states of Utah, Arizona, New Mexico, and Colorado in the USA).

Resin canal: Specialized, elongated cells that produce and store oleogum-resin in conifer trees and other oleogum-resin producing trees.

Axial (AX-ē-all) resin canal: Vertical, elongated cells running the length of a tree that produce and store oleogum-resin in conifer trees.

Radial (RAY-dē-all) resin canal: Horizontal, elongated cells radiating from the central heartwood that produce and store oleogum-resin in conifer trees.

Pitch blister: External, horizontally elongated bark cells containing oleogum-resin on fir trees.

DR. WOOLLEY'S CHALLENGE

- Draw a simple diagram of the side perspective of a 50-year-old pine tree. Include the root mass in the soil. Circle and label the Air Domain and Soil Domain. Label the required 5 inputs and 4 outputs for plant growth.
- Explain to a child or adult how oleogum-resin exudes from axial resin canals, radial resin canals, and resin blisters on trees to protect them from bacterial decay and to heal wounds.

5

Plants are Intelligent

You may have wondered how plants seem to know how to grow and defend themselves. How do they know how to produce 200 different molecules in their essential oil? After all, plants do not have cranial brains like humans, grasshoppers, butterflies, dogs, horses, robins, deer, squirrels, parrots, and beavers. So do plants have the ability to think? Do plants have intelligence?

This chapter will help you feel educated and intelligent while answering such questions as:

> "How does a peppermint plant know how to create essential oil molecules?"
>
> "How does a lavender seed know how to grow into a lavender bush?"

Plants are intelligent. They know how to produce essential oil molecules in Hair-like trichomes. They know how to produce viable seeds that can replicate their species. They know how to attract bees and butterflies to pollinate their flowers. They know how to grow tall from a little seed. Plants do all of this automatically without having to think. I refer to this knowledge as **plant intelligence.** This plant intelligence is found in the plant's seed. Every seed contains the complete instructions necessary for a tree, bush, or plant to grow and produce additional seeds. That is intelligence!

PLANT DNA IS PLANT INTELLIGENCE

Plant intelligence is bundled in the central nucleus of each plant cell and in every seed. These bundles are called **DNA** (**D**ioxyribo**N**ucleic **A**cid). Plant DNA is similar to human DNA in terms of its function. DNA is made up of two parallel **macromolecules** (large molecules). Each cell contains a copy of DNA specific to the plant species. There are numerous bundles of DNA molecules in each cell. All the intelligence and know-how for a plant to grow, produce essential oil molecules, produce colors on their leaves and flowers, and create leaf patterns is contained in its DNA molecules.

The DNA macromolecule is composed of four biochemical building blocks called nucleotides: adenine (A), thymine (T), cytosine (C), and guanine (G). These small nucleotide building blocks look like rungs on a long, twisted ladder. The two, long side-poles represent two adjacent DNA strands. A pair of interacting nucleotides act like rungs on the ladder to connect the two side-poles.

Let's Build a DNA Ladder. I want you to understand the basic design of a DNA **double helix** (meaning a pair of parallel spirals) macromolecule. It will help you understand how plant intelligence is packed in every seed. Observe that the DNA molecule looks like a twisted, wooden ladder. I would like you to look at the parts of the DNA ladder as if it were a wooden ladder.

A wooden ladder can be divided in two by sawing through the center of each rung. Each of the two side-poles with half-rungs sticking out represents half of the DNA double helix molecule. Each half-rung represents one of the nucleotide building block molecules (A, T, C, or G) that make up the side-pole. In this example each half-rung of one side-pole is labeled with the letters A, T, C, or G.

Now look at the corresponding half-rungs on the opposite side-pole. They are labeled following two simple rules. First, if the half-rung of the first side-pole is labeled A, then its matching half-rung on the opposite side-pole is always T; and visa-versa. Second, if the half-rung is labeled C, then its matching half-rung on the opposite side-pole is always G; and visa-versa. This way there are only four matching possibilities: A-T, T-A, C-G, and G-C. This is part of the biochemical intelligence stored in plant cells.

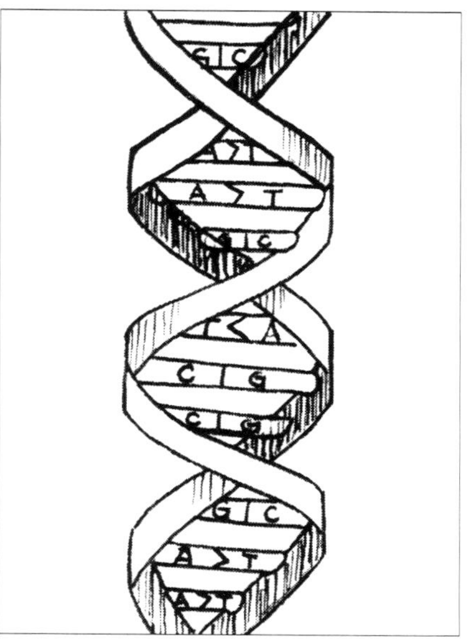

Figure 14. Diagram of DNA double helix macromolecule showing A-T and G-C pairings of nucleotides.

To complete the DNA double helix the corresponding half-rungs must be connected. This will create the double spiral image. The A-T and T-A linkages are made with two biochemical interactions. The C-G and G-C rungs are stronger because there are three biochemical interactions that hold them together. These interactions are like taping together the half-rungs on a sawed ladder.

The DNA design rules applied in making DNA double helix macromolecules is the source of the plant intelligence. The series of A, T, C, G nucleotides locked in the DNA design are the codes used to operate every living cell and produce essential oil molecules.

DNA is like a Twisted Ladder. The two strands of DNA are attracted to each other by pairing the A-T and C-G nucleotides. Combining millions of these A-T and C-G attractions keeps the two strands of DNA closely associated, but NOT permanently linked. The twisting of the two strands of DNA into a double helix helps reduce the length and size of the DNA strands.

DNA is a list of Instructions to build proteins. The consecutive sequence of nucleotides (e.g., T,T,G,A,T,T,A,C,A,T,T) on a relatively small portion of the DNA molecule chain contains instructions to build **protein** molecules within the cell. Protein molecules are important to the functioning health of plant cells. There are millions of different proteins in each plant. Some proteins are used to build structures, some are used as messenger molecules, and others are used to promote biochemical reactions. Protein molecules help produce essential oil molecules.

DNA helps plants adapt to their environment. Incidental changes to the nucleotide sequence of DNA occur from time-to-time when cells replicate and divide. Cell replication occurs when plants grow. Instead of a nucleotide sequence such as T,T,G,A,T,**T**,A,C,A,T,T, a small change like T,T,G,A,T,**A**,A,C,A,T,T can result by substituting A for T. These incidental changes are called **genetic mutations.** Most mutations do not have a major effect on the health of the cell or the plant.

Some genetic mutations actually help individual plants adapt to changing environmental conditions, like colder, warmer, wetter, or drier climates. Some mutations weaken the individual plant. The plants that adapt best to changes in their environment survive and thrive. This demonstrates how plants use their DNA design to intelligently adapt to environmental changes.

BUILDING PROTEINS USING CODES FROM DNA

Since cells produce essential oil molecules, it will be helpful to be familiar with the major parts of plant cells. All living operations within a plant cell depend on the intelligence of its DNA macromolecules. The intelligent DNA macromolecules are locked up in the **nucleus,** or the central core of each cell. Outside the spherical cell nucleus is a region called the cell **cytoplasm,** a busy factory where biochemical molecules and essential oil molecules are constructed. The cytoplasm is surrounded by the outer cell **membrane.**

Protein molecules are produced in the cell cytoplasm and play a key life-keeping role. Protein molecules help the cell operate efficiently. It takes thousands of different types of protein molecules to keep a cell alive. It takes hundreds of specialized proteins to construct essential oil molecules.

Here is how the DNA intelligence works. DNA molecules must remain in the cell nucleus. A messenger molecule carrying a copy of the DNA information is needed to start the protein-building process. This process for copying the DNA instructions is called **transcription.** This one-stranded copy of the DNA instructions is called **Messenger RNA** (**R**ibo**N**ucleic **A**cid). This Messenger RNA molecule can migrate from the cell nucleus to the cell cytoplasm, acting as a messenger for DNA.

Once the Messenger RNA molecule is in the cell cytoplasm, it can begin the process of building protein molecules, a process

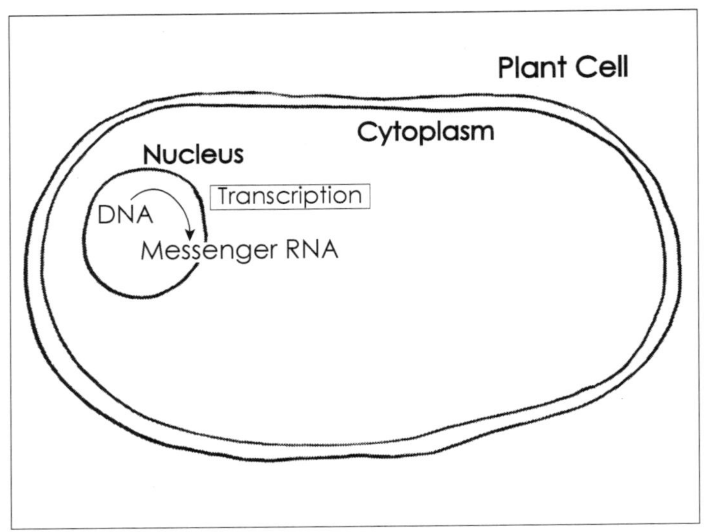

Figure 15. Plant cell depicting DNA and Messenger RNA molecules in cell nucleus.

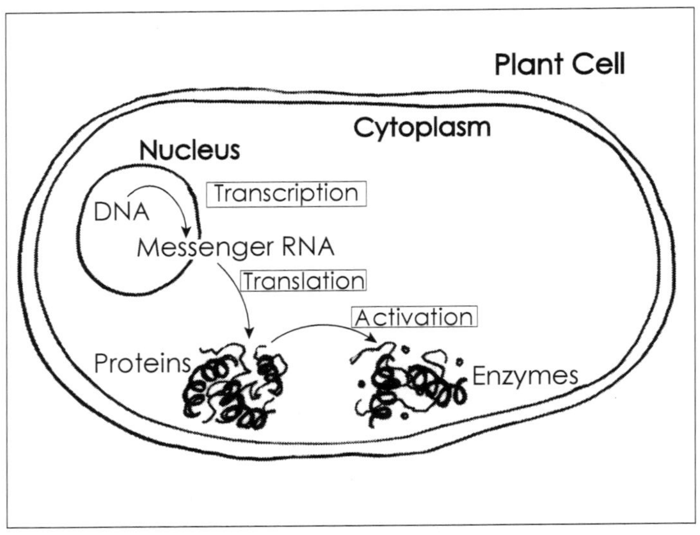

Figure 16. Plant cell depicting the translation of Messenger RNA molecule to produce protein and enzyme molecules.

known as **translation.** The Messenger RNA molecule contains all the instructions for constructing proteins. Proteins are composed of chains containing approximately 100-800 **amino acid** molecules. The intelligence of plant DNA molecules is demonstrated by building thousands of different protein molecules. Here are the basic steps:

1. The 2-strand DNA macromolecule residing in the cell nucleus or seed contains all the intelligence to make the plant grow.
2. A DNA molecule temporarily unzips its double helix structure in order to create a single-stranded copy called Messenger RNA (the process of transcription).
3. The Messenger RNA migrates out of the cell nucleus into the cell cytoplasm.
4. The Messenger RNA is decoded segment-by-segment and translated into building a protein molecule (the process of translation).

ENZYMES HELP BUILD ESSENTIAL OIL MOLECULES

All the intelligent instructions for building essential oil molecules are contained in the DNA molecules. Some protein molecules are designed for specific functions in the biochemical manufacturing cytoplasm. These efficiency-oriented proteins are called **enzymes.**

Enzymes play a key function in the biochemical pathways that produce essential oil molecules. Enzymes help facilitate biochemical reactions at lower-than-expected energy costs. Enzymes act like shortcuts from beginning to end, cutting out unnecessary biochemical reactions. Enzymes save on the cost of ATP biochemical energy molecules. They are efficiency experts.

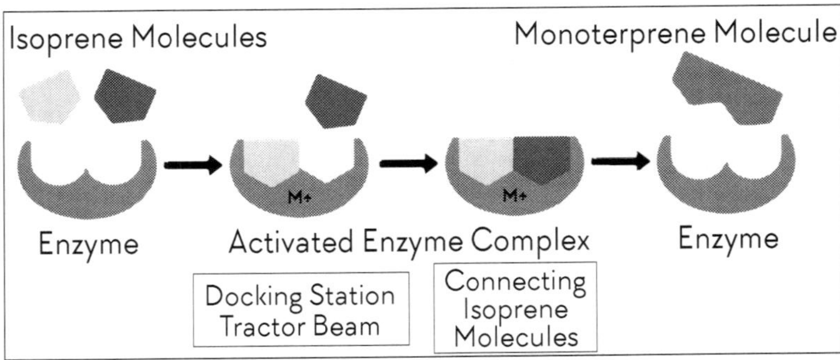

Figure 17. The production of essential oil Monoterpene molecule with the help of an activated enzyme-mineral complex.

Enzymes act like **biochemical docking stations** for assembling essential oil molecules. In addition, enzymes possess a **biochemical tractor beam** that attracts the essential oil building block molecules. Adding a mineral atom to a protein molecule transforms it into an enzyme, a process known as **enzyme activation.** The mineral atom (such as zinc or magnesium) helps transform the shape of the docking station. The activated **enzyme-mineral complex** now acts as a powerful tractor beam for specific essential oil building blocks.

Here is how essential oil molecules are constructed with the help of enzyme molecules. The biochemical tractor beam may attract two essential oil building blocks into the docking station of the large enzyme molecule. Using ATP biochemical energy molecules the two small building blocks are fused together to make one larger essential oil molecule. Once the essential oil building blocks are permanently connected, the docking station opens and releases the new essential oil molecule. The enzyme molecule helped by quickly connecting the essential oil building blocks and performed the connection using fewer ATP biochemical energy molecules. The enzyme is now ready to repeat the cycle to produce more essential oil molecules.

There are specific enzymes for the creation of each essential oil molecule. There are hundreds of different enzymes to handle the production of the 100-300 different essential oil molecules produced in every plant. The production of these essential oil enzymes is all coded in the biochemical sequences of the DNA macromolecule.

HOW PLANT INTELLIGENCE WORKS

DNA is the intelligence within the plant. Let's review the intelligent processes starting with DNA and ending with essential oil molecules.

1. The 2-strand DNA macromolecule residing in the cell nucleus or seed contains all the intelligence to make the plant grow.
2. A DNA molecule temporarily unzips its double helix structure in order to create a single-stranded copy called Messenger RNA (the process of transcription).
3. The Messenger RNA migrates out of the cell nucleus into the cell cytoplasm.
4. The Messenger RNA is decoded segment-by-segment and translated into building a protein molecule (the process of translation).
5. The Protein molecule is activated by mineral atoms to become an enzyme-mineral complex (the process of activation).
6. The Activated Enzyme-mineral complex assists in connecting small building blocks into larger essential oil molecules (by using docking station and tractor beam functions).

I do not expect you to teach someone this process. I only want you to become familiar with the intelligent biochemical processes

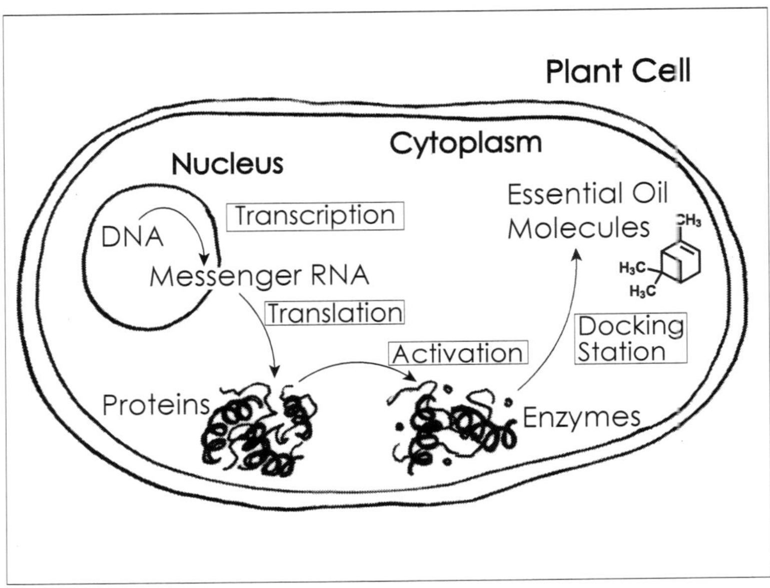

Figure 18. Plant cell depicting the abbreviated 5-step process for producing essential oil molecules as dictated by intelligent DNA instructions.

that all start with plant DNA. It is important that you understand that each lavender seed, each peppermint seed, and each frankincense seed has a copy of the DNA intelligence to generate a growing plant and essential oil molecules for that species. The seed contains all the intelligence to grow leaves, flowers, seeds, and essential oil molecules.

QUIET INTELLIGENCE™ AND ACTIVE INTELLIGENCE™

Plants may not be able to think like humans and animals, but they are "smart". I refer to the DNA instructions as **Quiet Intelligence™.** Quiet Intelligence is the sequence of DNA nucleotides that translates to produce proteins, makes cells function, helps cells produce energy, and determines lifespan. Quiet Intelligence functions like a computer program, performing functions it is only programmed to do. All organisms in the Plant Kingdom possess Quiet Intelligence.

The DNA macromolecule demonstrates Quiet Intelligence because it functions without conscious thought. It automatically functions to keep plants alive. Each plant within a species has similar (but not the same) Quiet Intelligence. Each plant within a species is an individual with unique, inherited Quiet Intelligence. Animals and humans also possess Quiet Intelligence because of their inherited DNA from their parents.

Animals and humans possess an additional source of intelligence. The Animal Kingdom includes insects, sea animals, birds, land animals, and humans. Animals possess a thinking cerebral brain that store memories and are capable of making survival choices. I refer to this cerebral thinking as **Active Intelligence™.** Active Intelligence records experiences with other animals, cause-and-effect relationships, emotions, past-memories, and provides for verbal and non-verbal communications.

Active Intelligence helps animals and humans in making choices, like what foods to eat, what foods to avoid, whom to make friends with, where to sleep, how to avoid being eaten, and thousands of additional survival choices. A species' capacity for Active Intelligence is determined by its inherited DNA instructions.

Every human is an individual with similar and unique Quiet Intelligence, yet the Active Intelligence they possess is determined by his or her own life experiences. Some individuals are more intelligent than others. Your DNA is just as sophisticated and complex as the DNA of plants; they produce proteins, enzymes, cells, tissues, and blood cells to keep you healthy. Your brain does not make your DNA function. Your DNA is an automatic intelligence, your Quiet Intelligence, which subconsciously works all day, every day, to keep your body running.

PLANT SPECIES

All plant species (e.g., oregano, spearmint, pine, etc.) contain unique DNA instructions. Every seed contains a copy of the DNA instructions unique to that species. Lavender plants will always produce lavender seeds. Lavender seeds will always sprout lavender plants. Lavender plants will always produce lavender essential oil.

A lavender seed produces lavender essential oil according to its DNA instructions. A lavender seed originating from France contains all the Quiet Intelligence within its DNA to produce lavender essential oil wherever it is grown. A French lavender seed planted in southern France, Bulgaria, western China, western USA, or Spain will produce lavender essential oil of similar, but slightly different quality. Any slight differences in quality are associated with differences in soil, geology, and climate. As long as the growing conditions are favorable and similar, the quality of the lavender essential oil will be similar. The DNA instructions within the lavender seed for producing lavender essential oil molecules are followed from start to finish. That is the Quiet Intelligence found in every seed of lavender.

Every aromatic plant species produces a unique set of essential oil molecules. A set of 100-300 essential oil molecules is typical for every aromatic plant species. Some essential oil molecules, like limonene, may be found in numerous, unrelated species, such as in orange, ylang ylang, and geranium essential oils. Each plant species has a unique set of DNA instructions to construct enzymes for producing a unique set of essential oil molecules. This DNA difference allows scientists to classify plant species by plant structure, plant essential oil molecules, plant proteins, plant enzymes, and plant DNA.

Plant Individuals. Each plant within a species is unique. That means there are very few exact duplicates (e.g., twins, triplets) in the wild. Nearly all Boswellia sacra frankincense trees growing in

Oman and Yemen are individuals with slight differences. Each individual plant has a slightly different branch structure, leaf structure, leaf number, flower color, and DNA. The only way to get DNA-duplicates of a plant is by propagating a **plant cutting,** a plant that grows from the root of another plant, or by **embryo cloning.** In a field of lavender, every plant is slightly different; yet quite similar.

The sharing of DNA molecules between plants creates individuals with unique characteristics. Since plants are not mobile, they require insects, birds, and animals to pollinate and share pollen grains from one plant to another. The pollen grains contain individualized DNA instructions that combine with the DNA instructions in the pollinated flower to produce a unique set of DNA instructions in their seeds. Each seed on a frankincense tree contains similar, yet slightly unique DNA instructions. Just as all humans are similar but unique, plants within the same species are also similar yet unique individuals.

Individual plants produce a unique composition of essential oil molecules as a result of their distinct DNA instructions. Harvesting thousands of peppermint plants provides an average composition for each batch of peppermint essential oil. The average composition of each batch of peppermint essential oil will be slightly different from the previous batches, but the difference is only marginal and usually not noticeable without expensive laboratory testing.

PLANTS ARE INTELLIGENT

Are plants intelligent? Yes indeed! They know how to produce essential oil molecules because of their Quiet Intelligence. Plants do not have a brain like humans, but their DNA is very sophisticated and complex.

It requires considerable intelligence to convert Carbon Dioxide molecules from the air and water molecules from the soil into growing leaves, stems, fruit, and producing essential oil molecules. Plant intelligence is the basis for essential oil production.

Quiet Intelligence is the set of DNA instructions that govern the operation of each cell. These instructions are like memories because they are passed on from generation-to-generation in the DNA macromolecules. Generations of lavender plants have grown from seed, survived harsh environments, and produced lavender essential oil molecules. All of this knowledge and experience is wrapped up in the lavender DNA macromolecules. That is what makes lavender plants, and all plants, so intelligent.

I simplified plant biochemistry so I could give you a taste for plant intelligence. If you want to know more details, pick up a textbook in the library or second-hand bookstore about cell biology or plant physiology. You can find out more about the processes of DNA transcription, Messenger RNA translation, and enzyme activation by searching for these terms on the internet. Regardless how much you learn about plant biochemistry you will always come to the same conclusion: plants are intelligent.

EXPLORING SUMMARY

- The intelligence of plants is found in their cellular DNA macromolecules.
- The sequence of DNA nucleotides represents the intelligence of plants.
- Plant intelligence is passed from generation-to-generation by the DNA macromolecules.
- The biochemical codes found in the DNA molecules control plant growth and construction of essential oil molecules.
- Quiet Intelligence™ is the term that describes the automatic control that DNA dictates for each plant cell.
- Active Intelligence™ is the term that describes the selected choices that animals and humans make based on recalled experiences stored in their cerebral brains.

- DNA macromolecules code for the production of cellular proteins and enzymes that control the health of each plant, animal, and human cell.
- The Quiet Intelligence of DNA controls the construction of all 100-300 different essential oil molecules that make up a plant's essential oil.

GLOSSARY

Plant Intelligence: The concept that plants "know" how to grow, interact with their external environment, and communicate using essential oil molecules.

DNA: The abbreviation of DioxyriboNucleic Acid. DNA is a chain of connected nucleotide molecules, composed of two-strands of DNA in a double helix formation. DNA is the inherited Quiet Intelligence of plants and animals.

Macromolecule: Any extremely large molecules built by connecting smaller molecules into a long chain.

Nucleotide: A set of 4 biochemical building blocks (abbreviated A, T, C, G) that connect into chains to produce DNA macromolecules and Messenger RNA.

Double helix: Helix describes a spiral shape. Double helix is a close association of two spiral formations.

Protein: A chain of 100-800 amino acid molecules that form a large 3-dimensional structure. Proteins are defined as a chain of connected amino acids molecules.

Genetic mutation: A change in a DNA nucleotide sequence that occurs when cells replicate and divide. Mutations occur naturally and can improve the survival of individual plants.

Nucleus: The central core of each cell that contains a plant's DNA.

Cytoplasm: The liquid within the cell (excluding nucleus) where proteins, enzymes, and essential oils are constructed.

Membrane: The spherical lining that surrounds the nucleus is the nucleus membrane. The spherical lining that surrounds the cytoplasm is the outer cell membrane.

Transcription: The process of copying the nucleotide sequence of a DNA strand to form a single-stranded Messenger RNA macromolecule.

Messenger RNA: This single stranded RiboNucleic Acid is composed of nucleotides and is a copy of one strand of a DNA double helix. It contains the instructions to build protein molecules. It can travel (be a messenger for DNA) from the cell nucleus to the cell cytoplasm.

Translation: The process of decoding a sequence of three consecutive nucleotides on Messenger RNA chain and adding the appropriate amino acid molecule to a growing protein chain.

Amino Acid: An assortment of 20 biochemical building blocks to build protein molecules.

Enzyme: A protein activated by select mineral atoms. Enzymes facilitate biochemical reactions and control the biosynthesis of essential oil molecules.

Biochemical Docking Station: This is 3-dimensional space within an enzyme where essential oil building block molecules can fit.

Biochemical Tractor Beam: The attraction created by mineral atoms and the enzyme molecule to pull in essential oil building block molecules.

Enzyme Activation: The process of adding mineral atoms to specific regions of a protein to create a biochemical tractor beam.

Enzyme-Mineral Complex: Enzyme-mineral complexes form a biochemical docking station and biochemical tractor beam to attract essential oil building blocks and facility efficient construction of essential oil molecules.

Quiet Intelligence™: The DNA codes and instructions used to produce proteins, enzymes, and essential oil molecules. The DNA instructions that automatically control all biochemical processes within a cell to help a plant grow, survive, and thrive.

Active Intelligence™: The learned experiences stored and recalled by the cerebral brain of animals and humans to assist in making survival choices.

Plant cutting: The process of creating a DNA-identical plant by cutting and rooting a branch from a plant or tree.

Embryo cloning: The process of creating a DNA-identical plant using cell tissues in a test tube.

DR. WOOLLEY'S CHALLENGE

- Explain to a child or adult the difference between Active Intelligence and Quiet Intelligence.
- Use the words Active Intelligence and Quiet Intelligence in a conversation, email, or on social media.
- Describe to a child or adult how Quiet Intelligence of plants helps them produce essential oil molecules.
- Draw a rough diagram showing how DNA controls the production of essential oil molecules. Use the following words: Cell nucleus, Cell cytoplasm, DNA, Transcription, Messenger RNA, Translation, Proteins, Activation, Enzymes, docking station, tractor beam, and essential oil molecules.

6

Monoterpene Molecules

Water is a simple liquid that is composed of billions of just one molecule, H_20. You probably learned this fact early in life. When you first experienced the aroma of essential oils, it may have been normal to think, "Peppermint oil must be composed of just one molecule, the peppermint molecule." The irony is that there are many different molecules in each drop of essential oil.

Let us explore the aroma and structure of essential oil molecules. I will do my best to simplify the chemistry, show you the molecules, and describe their aromas. The purpose of this chapter is to open your mind to the wonder and simplicity of essential oil molecules.

Do not get bogged down or try to memorize all the molecules in the next six chapters (Monoterpenes, Oxygenated Monoterpenes, Sesquiterpenes, Diterpenes, Triterpenes, and Tetraterpenes). Skim through these six chapters to become familiar with essential oil molecules so you can understand the subsequent chapters. You can always come back to these six chapters to highlight more useful phrases.

PLANTS PRODUCE ESSENTIAL OIL MOLECULES

Plants use their DNA Quiet Intelligence™ to construct essential oil molecules using Carbon atoms from Carbon Dioxide gas and

Hydrogen atoms from water. There are two main biochemical pathways for connecting Carbon and Hydrogen atoms to construct essential oil molecules.

One pathway is called the Shikimate Pathway in which many essential oil molecules found in spice oils are produced. We are not going to explore this minor pathway. We will explore the Isoprene Pathway where thousands of the most common essential oil molecules are constructed.

The biochemistry of Isoprene Pathway is easy to understand because the molecules are constructed in groups of 5 Carbon atoms and 10 Carbon atoms. Yet there are 100-300 different molecules in every essential oil. How complex! I will make it simple.

ISOPRENE BUILDING BLOCKS

Plants use photosynthesized sugars to produce essential oil molecules. As instructed by their DNA, plants transform 6-Carbon sugar molecules into 5-Carbon isoprene molecules. This transformation uses several ATP biochemical energy molecules.

The 5-Carbon isoprene molecule is composed solely of Carbon atoms (C) and Hydrogen atoms (H). The numbers next to the Hydrogen atoms refers to how many are connected to the Carbon atom (i.e., CH3 means three Hydrogen atoms connected to one Carbon atom). The lines between the Carbon atoms represent chemical connections as single bonds (-) or double bonds (=). Double bonds store more energy for biochemical reactions.

Here is what you need to know about essential oil atoms and chemical bonds between the atoms. The Carbon atom always has four chemical bonds or connections. That requirement can be met in two ways. First, the Carbon atom can be connected to four different atoms (e.g., Carbon, Hydrogen, or Oxygen atoms) with four single bonds. Second, the Carbon atom can be connected to only three other atoms; one connection via a double bond and the other two connections via single bonds. The isoprene molecule contains both varieties of Carbon connections to three and four different atoms. Count the connections to the Carbon atoms in the isoprene molecule.

3 views of the isoprene molecule

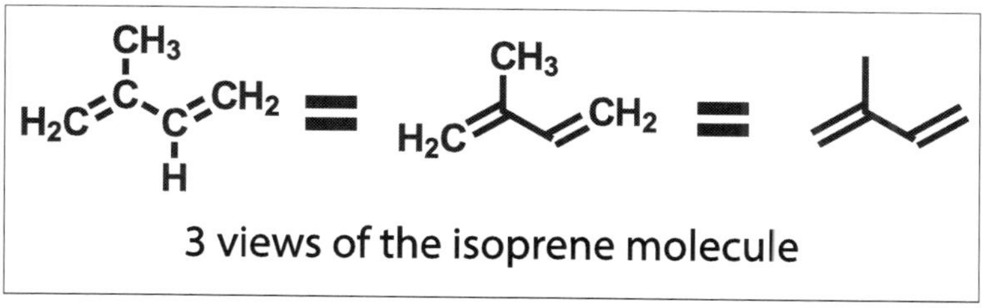

Figure 19. Three depictions of the atomic structure of the isoprene molecule.

Hydrogen atoms have only one connection, never two connections. Notice that in the isoprene molecules there is one example where 3 Hydrogen atoms are connected to 1 Carbon atom. When two isoprene molecules are connected (5 + 5 = 10) it is called a terpene unit. Terpene means "a 10-Carbon molecule."

Essential oil chemistry is easy to understand. In order to determine the size of an essential oil molecule, just count how many 10-Carbon terpene molecules it possesses. Terpene means "10-Carbon molecule." Plants know how to connect terpene molecules together to make larger molecules. It is all coded in the DNA to produce essential oil molecules.

Monoterpene means "one 10-Carbon molecule" (1 x 10 = 10).

Sesquiterpene means "one and a half 10-Carbon molecules" (1.5 x 10 = 15).

Diterpene means "two 10-Carbon molecules" (2 x 10 = 20).

Triterpene means "three 10-Carbon molecules" (3 x 10 = 30).

Tetraterpene means "four 10-Carbon molecules (4 x 10 = 40).

Plant DNA controls the biochemical processes that construct

hundreds of different essential oil molecules from the isoprene and terpene building blocks. There are hundreds of ways to connect the 5-Carbon isoprene and 10-Carbon terpene building blocks that yield hundreds of unique essential oil molecules.

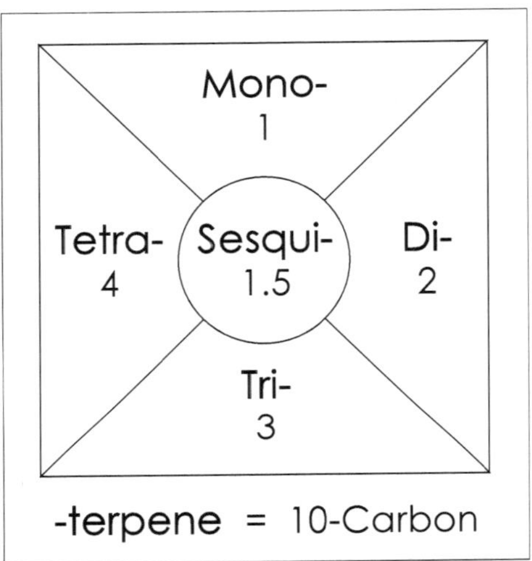

Figure 20. A schematic representation of the prefixes and suffixes of essential oil terpene molecules.

MONOTERPENES

These 10-Carbon essential oil molecules are prepared by linking two isoprene molecules. "Mono-" means "one" and "-terpene" means "10-Carbon molecule". All **Monoterpenes** contain 10 Carbon atoms. There are hundreds of different Monoterpene molecules; each with a unique shape, each with a unique aroma, and each with its own biochemical activity.

Monoterpenes are composed solely of Carbon (C) and Hydrogen (H) atoms; usually with 10 Carbon atoms and 16 Hydrogen atoms. You may also hear Monoterpenes referred to as hydrocarbons. The term hydrocarbon simply means molecules composed solely of Hydrogen and Carbon atoms.

Frankincense (Boswellia carterii) essential oil from Somalia is composed of numerous Monoterpene molecules. About 80% of the molecules in frankincense essential oil are Monoterpenes. The alpha-pinene molecule is responsible for a third of all the molecules in frankincense essential oil. The aroma of alpha-pinene is said by most people to be "piney". The limonene molecule makes up 13% of all the molecules in frankincense. Limonene has a strong "sweet, citrus, orange" aroma combination. The alpha-thujene molecule makes up 12% of the frankincense components and has a "woody, green, herbal" aroma combination. The remaining Monoterpene molecules add variety to the aroma of frankincense essential oil.

Frankincense Essential Oil Monoterpenes	**Content %**
alpha-thujene	12.6%
alpha-pinene	30.5%
camphene	1.1%
Sabinene	5.5%
beta-pinene	2.0%
Myrcene	5.5%
alpha-phellandrene	3.3%
cis-4-carene	1.2%
para-cymene	4.9%
carvomenthene	0.2%
Limonene	13.5%
cis-beta-ocimene	0.2%
gamma-terpinene	0.5%
para-cymenene	0.2%
alpha-terpinolene	0.1%
Perillene	0.2%
Total	**81.5%**

Molecule Skeletal Structures. The molecules illustrated in this book are represented as skeletal structures. Carbon atoms are at the junction where two lines meet. Each line represents the connecting chemical bond, whether single (-) or double (=). Hydrogen atoms are not shown in these skeletal structures except as depicted at the ends of molecules.

I like skeletal structure representations because it shows the difference between molecules. This is fundamental in understanding essential oil chemistry because <u>shape and structure determines the aroma of the molecule.</u> Two molecules of exactly the same number of Carbon and Hydrogen atoms but in <u>different 3-dimensional arrangements</u> will emit two distinct aromas.

There are hundreds of different Monoterpene molecules each with its own unique structure and shape. Some Monoterpenes, like myrcene and cis-beta-ocimene, look like a long chain of Carbon atoms. They are referred to as **Acyclic Monoterpenes** because **they do not form a ring of Carbon atoms.**

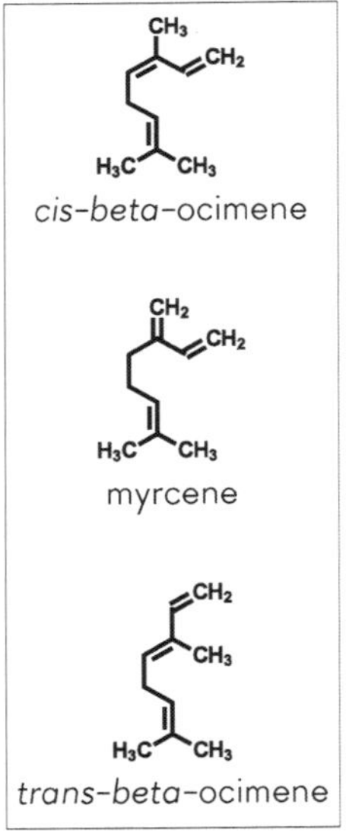

Figure 21. Biochemical structures of Acyclic Monoterpene molecules.

The molecules limonene and terpinolene have a cyclic structure forming a ring of Carbon atoms. They are referred to as Cyclic Monoterpenes.

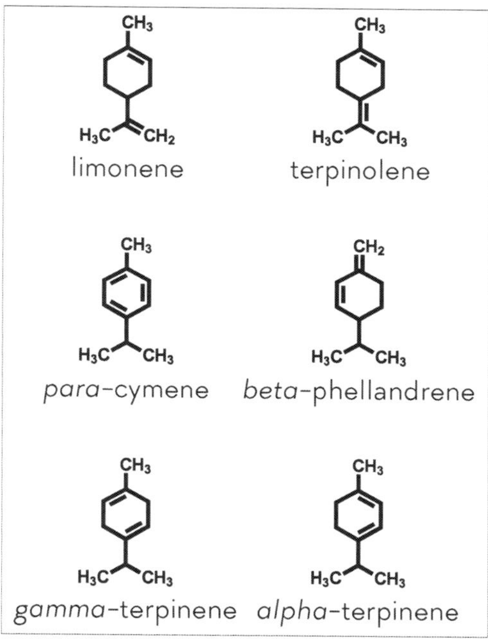

Figure 22. Biochemical structures of Cyclic Monoterpene molecules.

Some Monoterpenes, like alpha-pinene and sabinene, are referred to as Bicyclic Monoterpenes because they possess two (bi-) circular structures in the molecules.

Scientists have identified approximately 1000 different Monoterpene structures found in the essential oils of the Plant Kingdom. Every Monoterpene molecule possesses a unique structure, shape, and aroma. Each Monoterpene molecule has a different chemical arrangement of Carbon atoms, Hydrogen atoms, and chemical bonds.

Monoterpenes have unique properties. They are lightweight molecules, which causes them to evaporate quickly into the air.

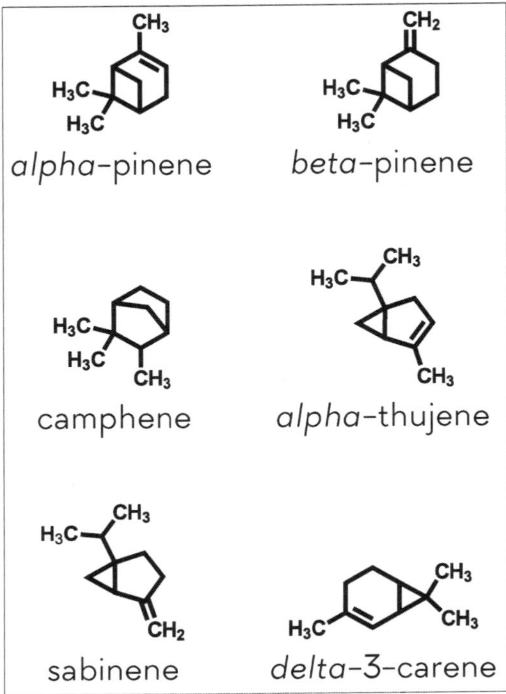

Figure 23. Biochemical structures of Bicyclic Monoterpene molecules.

Because the molecules randomly and rapidly move about in the air, they are often referred to as the "first aromas." They also dissipate quickly so they can also be thought of as "fleeting aromas."

Monoterpenes have a high propensity to penetrate into household objects. They penetrate and remain in wall paint, gypsum wall board, wooden cupboards, plastic dishes and utensils, carpeting and upholstery, and even ceramics and tiles. Your home absorbs the aromas of Monoterpene molecules when you diffuse essential oils. Fortunately these molecules eventually release from the home structure and re-enter the air.

Monoterpenes are great at dissolving and removing grease, like those found in kitchens, laundries, and bathrooms. Grease molecules are mostly hydrocarbon in composition so they readily dissolve in Monoterpenes. When little children mark the wall with crayons or markers, try cleaning the area with essential oils rich in Monoterpenes. Orange and lemon oils are rich in limonene (a Monoterpene) that makes them great degreasing agents. They also leave a refreshing aroma for everyone to enjoy.

Nearly every Monoterpene molecule has its own unique aroma. The sensitive olfactory nerve endings located in your nose detect the structure of each Monoterpene molecules, then sends a corresponding "aroma" signal to the brain. I associate a Monoterpene molecule to a key, and olfactory nerve endings to different locks. Keys are mobile, while locks have fixed locations. When the correct key fits into a lock, then an "aroma" signal is sent to the brain saying, "Hey, you just smelled a certain Monoterpene molecule".

The aromas of Monoterpene molecules tend to be described as "piney", "herbal", "woody", "citrusy", "sweet", "floral", or "spicy". Each Monoterpene has a unique aroma due to the unique structure and 3-dimensional shape. Most molecules possess about 3-5 aroma descriptors because different parts of their chemical structure fit into different olfactory nerve endings. The first descriptor is the dominant aroma. For instance, *beta*-pinene has a dominant "woody" aroma. It is as if three different portions of a Monoterpene molecule act as three different keys that can open three different locks (e.g., the "sweet" lock, the "citrusy" lock, and the "floral" lock for the limonene molecule). Here are some examples.

- myrcene = "spicy, piney, woody"
- ocimene = "tropical, green, piney"
- limonene = "sweet, citrus, orange"
- terpinolene = "fresh, woody, piney"
- *alpha*-pinene = "piney, woody, herbal"
- *beta*-pinene = "woody, piney, cooling"
- sabinene = "woody, spicy, citrus"

As you can see, the aroma of Monoterpene molecules is as varied as the chemical structure, despite having the same number of Carbon atoms.

Essential oils that predominantly contain more than 50% Monoterpenes belong to five diverse groups: Citrus oils, Wood oils, Oleogum-resin oils, Spice oils, and Perennial oils.

Citrus Oils. The Citrus oils commonly include orange, lemon, lime, tangerine, grapefruit, mandarin, yuzu, blood orange, bitter orange, and bergamot. These oils are cold-pressed from the peel of the citrus fruit during the juicing process.

Wood Oils. The Wood oils are generally steam distilled from scrap wood chips from the lumber milling process. The most common wood essential oils are balsam fir, black spruce, pine, hemlock, white fir, tsuga, cypress, thuja, Douglas fir, and juniper.

Oleogum-resin Oils. The Oleogum-resin oils are typically hydro-distilled, meaning the oleogum-resin is boiled in water to release the essential oil. The common Oleogum-resin essential oils are elemi, galbanum, myrrh, and frankincense.

Spice Oils. The Spice oils are predominantly cultivated to harvest fresh herbs and dried spices. Spice oils are usually steam distilled. The common Spice oils are nutmeg, tarragon, thyme, marjoram, caraway, cumin, dill, valerian, and celery seed.

Perennial Oils. The Perennial oils are usually the leafy material of perennial plants and bushes that are steam distilled. The most common ones are fleabane, goldenrod, cistus, angelica, myrtle, hyssop, ledum, yarrow, spearmint, and eucalyptus.

MONOTERPENE MOLECULES ARE COMMON

You will find Monoterpene molecules in nearly every essential oil. In general, they are the most abundant molecules in the essential oils of the Plant Kingdom. Monoterpene molecules are usually the first aroma that you detect. The molecules are small. They quickly and abundantly escape into the air. Most of the larger molecules in essential oils are built from Monoterpene molecules.

EXPLORING SUMMARY

- The basic building block unit of essential oil molecules is the 5-Carbon isoprene molecule composed of Carbon and Hydrogen atoms.
- Monoterpene molecules are assembled by connecting 5-Carbon isoprene molecules and 10-Carbon terpene molecules.
- Essential oils that contain at least 50% Monoterpene molecules make up five groups: Citrus oils, Wood oils, Oleogum-resin oils, Spice oils, and Perennial oils.
- Monoterpene molecules tend to have a "piney", "herbal", "woody", "citrusy", "sweet", "floral", or "spicy" aroma.

GLOSSARY

Isoprene Pathway: The biochemical process for building large essential oil molecules by connecting isoprene units. Also referred to as Non-Mevalonate Pathway, MEP Pathway, and DOXP Pathway.

Isoprene: A 5-Carbon molecule used as a building block to assemble larger essential oil molecules.

Terpene: Referring to a 10-Carbon molecule.

Monoterpene: A 10-Carbon essential oil molecule formed by connecting 2 isoprene units into 1 terpene unit. "Mono-" means "one" and "-terpene" means "10-Carbon molecule".

Acyclic (Ā-sigh-click) Monoterpene: A 10-Carbon essential oil hydrocarbon molecule that is linear, not cyclic.

Cyclic (SIGH-click) Monoterpene: A 10-Carbon essential oil hydrocarbon molecule that contains one cyclic ring of Carbon atoms.

Bicyclic (BUY-sigh-click) Monoterpene: A 10-Carbon essential oil hydrocarbon molecule that contains two cyclic rings of Carbon atoms.

DR. WOOLLEY'S CHALLENGE

- Make a list of some properties of Monoterpene molecules (e.g., small size, "first aroma", etc.).
- Make a list and describe to a child or adult the five groups of Monoterpene essential oils: Citrus oils, Wood oils, Oleogum-resin oils, Spice oils, and Perennial oils. Name two essential oils from each group.
- Draw or copy the structure of 5 Monoterpene molecules.
- Explain to a child or adult that the shape of Monoterpene molecules determines their aroma.

7

Oxygenated Monoterpene Molecules

Oxygenated Monoterpenes are very similar to Monoterpenes but with a little something extra to make them special. There adjective **Oxygenated** refers to adding an Oxygen atom to the Monoterpene molecule. These **Oxygenated Monoterpenes** still contain 10-Carbon atoms in the main structure, but with the addition of 1 or 2 Oxygen atoms. Many scientists call them **Terpenoids** (meaning "like terpenes") but I prefer to call them Oxygenated Monoterpenes.

There are different ways to incorporate the Oxygen (O) atom into the Monoterpene structure. That is because the Oxygen atom has only two bond connections. The Oxygen atom can connect with either one double bond (=) to a Carbon atom (C=O) or with two single bonds (-) to either two Carbon atoms (C-O-C) or a Carbon plus Hydrogen atoms (C-O-H).

There are six major classes of Oxygenated Monoterpenes that are defined by the way the Oxygen atom is connected: Alcohols (C-O-H), Aldehydes (-HC=O), Ketones (>C=O), Esters (-O-C=O), Ethers (C-O-C), and Oxides (C-O-C triangle). Each class of Oxygenated Monoterpenes has its own unique aroma and biochemical properties.

The aroma of Oxygenated Monoterpenes is a function of their shape and structure. The Oxygen atoms of neighboring

Frankincense Essential Oil Oxygenated Monoterpenes	Content %
myrcenol	0.2%
beta-thujone	0.3%
alpha-camphonene aldehyde	0.3%
trans-limonene oxide	0.1%
trans-pinocarveol	0.5%
cis-verbenol	0.6%
pinocamphone	0.2%
alpha-phellandren-8-ol	0.4%
para-cymen-8-ol	0.2%
terpinen-4-ol	1.9%
alpha-terpineol	0.6%
verbenone	0.4%
carvone	0.2%
bornyl acetate	0.4%
Total	**6.3%**

Oxygenated Monoterpene molecules attract one another. This is why Oxygenated Monoterpene molecules linger longer in the liquid and in the air than Monoterpene molecules. When an Oxygen atom is incorporated into a Monoterpene molecule, it plays a principal role in determining shapes and aromas.

Oxygenated Monoterpene Alcohols. Some common Oxygenated Monoterpene Alcohols are citronellol, geraniol, and nerol (found in lemongrass and geranium), linalool and lavandulol (found in lavender, geranium, and cinnamon bark), menthol, neomenthol, isomenthol and neoisomenthol (found in peppermint), terpinen-4-ol (found in tea tree, lavender, and cypress), and *alpha*-terpineol (found in tea tree and lavender). Notice that all of the molecule names end in "–ol". In general, that is the scientific suffix for Alcohol molecules.

The Oxygen atom in Alcohols is inserted between a Carbon (C) atom and a Hydrogen (H) atom. It looks something like this C-O-H. The other three connections to the Carbon atom are typically connected to three different Carbon or Hydrogen atoms. The Oxygen and Hydrogen atoms in Alcohols like to interact with water (H_2O). This makes Alcohols more water-loving than most other Oxygenated Monoterpenes.

Oxygenated Monoterpene Alcohols tend to have aromas that can be described as "flowery", "sweet", or "fruity". Some common Oxygenated Monoterpene Alcohol molecules have aromas described as:

- linalool = "floral, citrus, sweet"
- lavandulol = "floral, waxy, herbal"
- citronellol = "floral, rose, sweet"
- menthol = "minty, cooling, clean"
- neomenthol = "mentholic, cooling, minty"
- geraniol = "floral, sweet, fruity"
- terpinen-4-ol = "woody, mentholic, citrus"

Essential oils with high percentages of Oxygenated Monoterpene Alcohols include: lavender, ylang ylang, neroli, petitgrain, coriander, palmarosa, citronella, carrot seed, eucalyptus citriodora, bay laurel, lavandin, lavender, rosalina, basil, peppermint, geranium, rose, Moroccan thyme, and thyme (linalool chemotype).

Oxygenated Monoterpene Aldehydes. Some common Oxygenated Monoterpene Aldehydes are *trans*-cinnamaldehyde (found in cinnamon bark and cassia bark), citronellal, neral, and geranial (found in lemongrass), and myrtenal (found in Roman chamomile). Scientists typically identify them with the suffixes "-al" or "aldehyde".

The Oxygen atom in Aldehydes is attached to a Carbon atom at the ends of a molecule via a double bond. It looks something

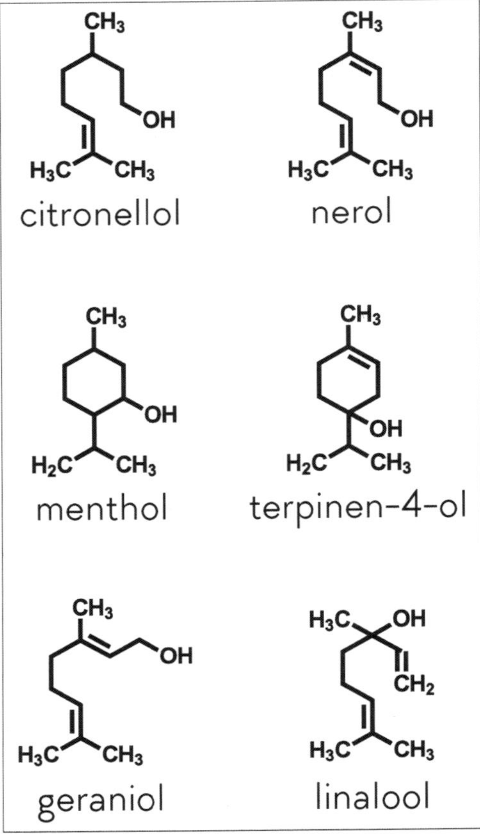

Figure 24. Biochemical structures of Oxygenated Monoterpene Alcohol molecules.

like this -HC=O. When you find the -HC=O at the end of a molecule, it is called an Aldehyde. The other connection to the Carbon atom is usually another Carbon atom.

Aldehydes provide a refreshing aroma to essential oils. Oxygenated Monoterpene Aldehydes are commonly described as "sweet", "floral", and "spicy". The aroma of some common Oxygenated Monoterpene Aldehydes are described as:

- *trans*-cinnamaldehyde = "cinnamon, sweet, spicy"
- citronellal = "sweet, floral, rose"
- neral = "lemon, sweet, citrus"
- geranial = "lemon, sweet, citrus"
- myrtenal = "sweet, cinnamon, spicy"

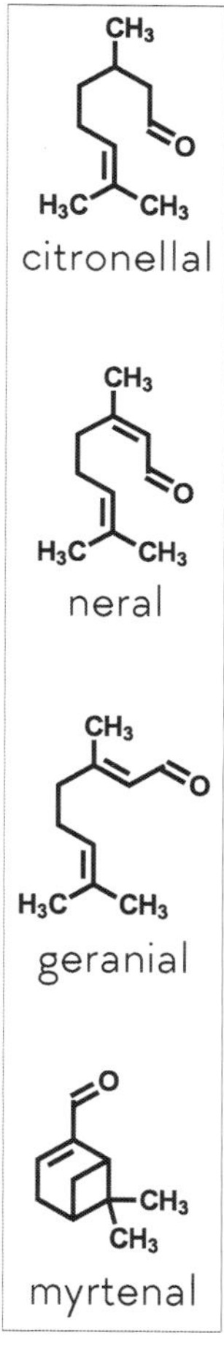

Figure 25. Biochemical structures of Oxygenated Monoterpene Aldehyde molecules.

Essential oils containing significant percentages of Oxygenated Monoterpene Aldehydes include cassia bark, cinnamon bark, cumin, lemongrass, xiang mao, palmarosa, citronella, eucalyptus citriodora, and melissa (lemon balm).

Oxygenated Monoterpene Ketones. Some common Oxygenated Monoterpene Ketones are menthone and isomenthone (found in peppermint, spearmint and geranium), carvone and verbenone (found in spearmint), piperitone (found in spearmint and peppermint), camphanone (found in rosemary and lavandin), dihydrocarvone (found in spearmint), and pulegone (found in peppermint).

The Oxygen atom in Ketones is similar to Oxygen atom in Aldehydes. A double bond connects the Oxygen and Carbon atoms somewhere in the middle of the molecule (not at the ends). Ketones are represented as >C=O for the Oxygenated functional group. Scientists refer to them as "ketone" or with the suffix "-one". The other two connections to the Carbon atom are usually to two different Carbon atoms.

The aromas of Oxygenated Monoterpene Ketones are generally described as "spicy", "minty", and "earthy". Some common Oxygenated Monoterpene Ketones and their aromas are:

- menthone = "minty, cooling, sweet"
- carvone = "spicy, minty, caraway"
- dihydrocarvone = "cooling, minty, woody"
- piperitone = "pungent, minty, peppermint"
- camphanone (camphor) = "camphorous, medicine, mothballs"
- verbenone = "spicy, minty, camphorous"

The essential oils that contain high percentages of Oxygenated Monoterpene Ketone molecules are peppermint, spearmint, cornmint, caraway, white camphor, davana, yarrow, calamus, helichrysum, eucalyptus dives, dill, sage, thuja, western red cedar, and hyssop.

Oxygenated Monoterpene Esters. Some common Oxygenated Monoterpene Esters in essential oils are found in Cinnamon bark

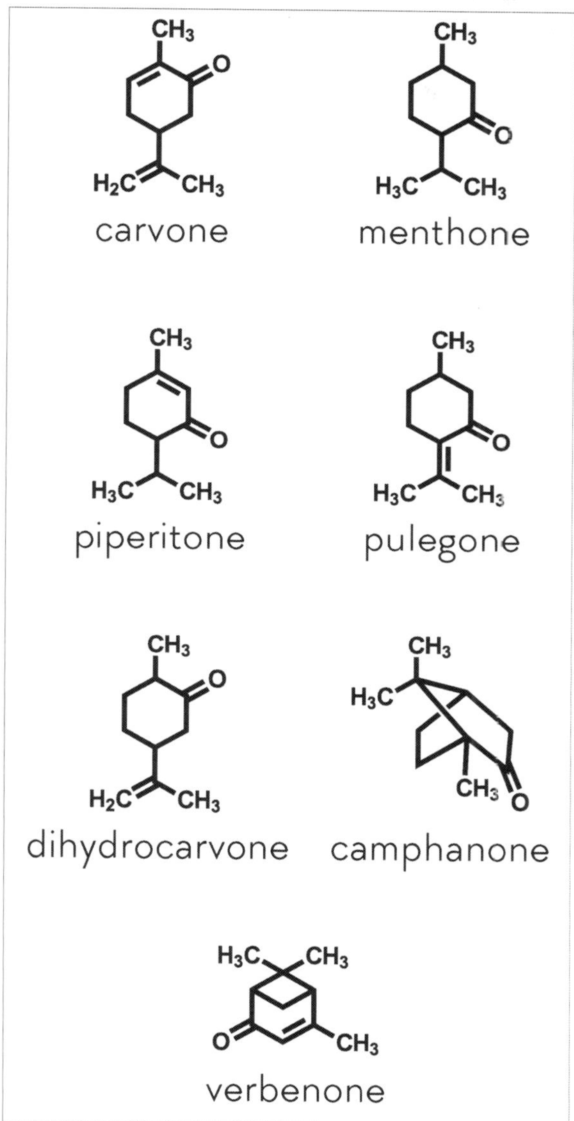

Figure 26. Biochemical structures of Oxygenated Monoterpene Ketone molecules.

oil include cinnamyl acetate and eugenyl acetate. Geranium contains the esters: citronellyl formate, geranyl formate, geranyl butyrate, and citronellyl butyrate. Helichrysum possesses neryl acetate. Lavender contains the esters: linalyl acetate and lavandulyl acetate.

Some of the most pleasurable aromas are found in Oxygenated Monoterpene Esters. Oxygenated Monoterpene Esters contain the basic 10-Carbon Monoterpene molecule, 2 Oxygen atoms, and an additional appendage possessing 1, 2, 3, 4, or 5 Carbon atoms. Scientists designate Esters using the suffix "-ate". Esters contain a central Carbon atom connected to two Oxygen atoms. One Oxygen atom is connected with a single bond (C-O) and the other Oxygen atom is connected with a double bond (C=O). Esters look something like this: O-C=O. The other connection to the Carbon atom is to another Carbon atom.

Esters are like two molecules put together (an alcohol molecule and a carboxylate molecule). Think of the carboxylate as the portion that contains the C=O and the alcohol portion containing the C-O. The Alcohol portion typically comes from the 10-Carbon Monoterpene molecule, while the added carboxylate portion is usually only 1, 2, 3, 4, or 5 Carbon atoms long. A 1-Carbon carboxylate portion is called "formate". The more common 2-Carbon carboxylate is called "acetate". The 3-Carbon carboxylate is known as "propionate", the 4-Carbon carboxylate is referred to as either called "butyrate" or "isobutyrate", and the 5-Carbon carboxylate is called "angelate."

Oxygenated Monoterpene Esters have very pleasant aromas. They are generally described as "fruity", "sweet", "floral", and "ripe". The aroma of common Oxygenated Monoterpene Esters include:

- cinnamyl acetate = "sweet, floral, cinnamon"
- neryl acetate = "floral, rose, sweet"
- linalyl acetate = "sweet, citrus, lavender"
- citronellyl formate = "sweet, fruity, peach"

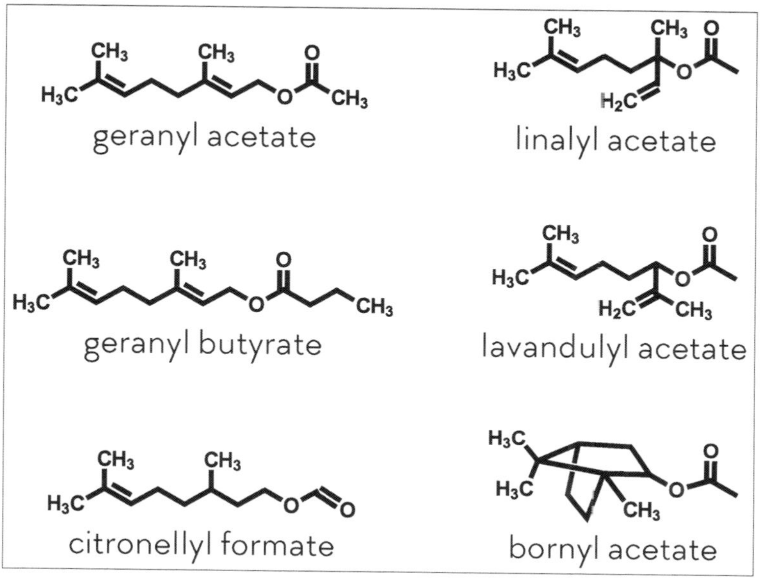

geranyl acetate

linalyl acetate

geranyl butyrate

lavandulyl acetate

citronellyl formate

bornyl acetate

Figure 27. Biochemical structures of Oxygenated Monoterpene Ester molecules.

Essential oils that contain high percentages of Oxygenated Monoterpene Esters are Roman chamomile, cinnamon bark, citronella, petitgrain, cardamom, helichrysum, bergamot, lavandin, jasmine, lemongrass, xiang mao, geranium, tsuga, valerian, black spruce, clary sage, and lavender.

These essential oils are regarded as "pleasant", "perfume-like", and "refreshing". Oxygenated Monoterpene Esters create the "sweet, floral, fruity" essential oils that you love so much.

Oxygenated Monoterpene Ethers and Oxides. One of the most common Oxygenated Monoterpene Ether molecules is 1,8-cineole (eucalyptol). Essential oils that contain significant percentages of Oxygenated Monoterpene Ether molecules (especially 1,8-Cineole) include eucalyptus (*Eucalyptus globulus*), lemon eucalyptus (*Eucalyptus citriodora*), blue mallee (*Eucalyptus polybractea*), eucalyptus radiata (*Eucalyptus radiata*), bay laurel, cajeput, niaouli, myrtle, ravensara, rosemary, cardamom, white camphor, thyme, sage, tea tree, rosemary, and Spanish marjoram.

Monoterpene Ethers and Oxides have the Oxygen atom sandwiched between two Carbon atoms. The shorthand scientific designation is C-O-C. What makes Oxygenated Monoterpene Oxides unique is that the two Carbon atoms are also connected, thereby forming a triangular shape. On the other hand, Oxygenated Monoterpene Ethers may have numerous Carbon atoms on each side of the Oxygen atom. In many Ether molecules, the Oxygen atom fits into a ring of 4, 5, or 6 Carbon atoms.

The aroma of 1,8-cineole is typically described as "eucalyptus". Oxygenated Monoterpene Ethers tend to provide a "minty" and "earthy" aroma. However, the aroma of many Oxygenated Monoterpene Ethers are also broadly described as "caramel", "rose", "pungent", "almond", and "floral".

Oxygenated Monoterpene Oxides are thought to form during the hot distillation process. The steam temperature is energetic enough to add an Oxygen atom to the double bond connecting two Carbon atoms. This results in the triangular shaped formation with two Carbon atoms and one Oxygen atom. Note that some molecules described with the "oxide" name are really Ethers (e.g., rose oxide and linalool oxide). Essential oils that contain Oxygenated Monoterpene Oxides include German chamomile, carrot seed, peppermint, cypress, hyssop, rose, geranium, and frankincense.

- 1,8-cineole = "eucalyptus, minty, fresh"
- 1,4-cineole = "cooling, pine, minty"
- rosefuran = "caramel, green, minty"
- menthofuran = "pungent, musty, nutty"
- furfural (ether and aldehyde) = "sweet, woody, almond"
- linalool oxide = "floral, woody, earthy"
- rose oxide = "green, rose, floral"

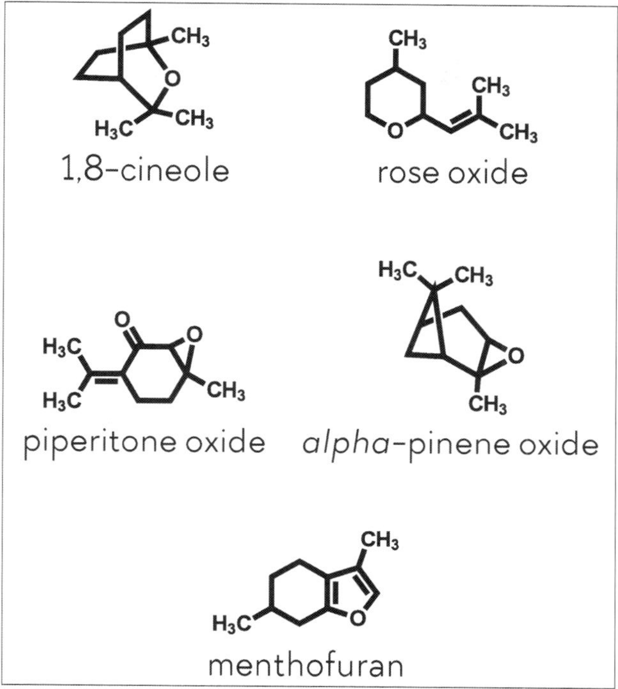

Figure 28. Biochemical structures of Oxygenated Monoterpene Ether and Oxide molecules.

Becoming familiar with the aroma and chemistry of Oxygenated Monoterpene molecules will help you understand the essential oils you use.

EXPLORING SUMMARY

- Plants produce Oxygenated Monoterpene molecules by adding 1 or 2 Oxygen atoms to 10-Carbon Monoterpene molecules.
- There are different classes of Oxygenated Monoterpene molecules referred to as Alcohols, Aldehydes, Ketones, Esters, Ethers, and Oxides.

- Monoterpene Alcohol molecules have a flowery aroma.
- Monoterpene Aldehyde molecules tend to have a "sweet", "floral", and "spicy" aroma.
- Monoterpene Ketone molecules tend to have a harsh aroma.
- Monoterpene Ester molecules have some of the sweetest aromas.
- Monoterpene Ether molecules have a "minty" and "earthy" aroma.

GLOSSARY

Oxygenated: When an Oxygen atom is added to a Monoterpene, Sesquiterpene, Diterpene, Triterpene, or Tetraterpene molecule. There are different classes referred to as Alcohol, Aldehyde, Ketone, Ester, Ether, or Oxide molecules.

Oxygenated Monoterpene: A 10-Carbon Monoterpene molecule possessing at least one Oxygen atom.

Terpenoid: Meaning "like a terpene" this is any of the Oxygenated Monoterpene molecules.

Oxygenated Monoterpene Alcohol: A 10-Carbon essential oil molecule containing one Oxygen atom sandwiched between a Carbon atom and a Hydrogen atom anywhere in the molecule (C-O-H).

Oxygenated Monoterpene Aldehyde: A 10-Carbon essential oil molecule containing one Oxygen atom connected to a Carbon atom with a double bond at a terminal end of the molecule (-HC=0).

Oxygenated Monoterpene Ketone: A 10-Carbon essential oil molecule containing one Oxygen atom connected to a Carbon atom with a double bond within the middle of the molecule (>C=0).

Oxygenated Monoterpene Ester: A 10-Carbon essential oil molecule containing two Oxygen atoms connected to a central Carbon atom in the middle of the molecule, one Oxygen atom connected with a single bond and the other with a double bond (O-C=O).

Oxygenated Monoterpene Oxide: A 10-Carbon essential oil molecule containing one Oxygen atom connected to two adjacent Carbon atoms to form a triangular shape in the molecule (C-O-C triangle).

Oxygenated Monoterpene Ether: A 10-Carbon essential oil molecule containing one Oxygen atom sandwiched between two Carbon atom chains in the middle of the molecule (C-O-C).

DR. WOOLLEY'S CHALLENGE

- Create a list and explain to a child or adult how an Oxygen atom can be added to Monoterpene molecules to form alcohols, aldehydes, ketones, esters, ethers, and oxides.
- Copy one molecule shape from each group: Monoterpene, Monoterpene alcohol, Monoterpene aldehyde, Monoterpene ketone, Monoterpene ester, Monoterpene ether, and Monoterpene oxide.
- Create a list of your favorite Oxygenated Monoterpene-rich essential oils.

8

Sesquiterpene Molecules

When plants connect a Monoterpene molecule (10 Carbon atoms) and an isoprene molecule (5 Carbon atoms), they produce a new molecule of 15 Carbon atoms known as a Sesquiterpene. "Sesqui-" means "one and a half" and "-terpene" means "10-Carbon molecule". I love Sesquiterpene-rich essential oils.

SESQUITERPENES

Sesquiterpene molecules contain 15 Carbon atoms and a number of Hydrogen atoms. They are classified as hydrocarbons just like Monoterpenes. It is estimated that about 5000 different Sesquiterpene molecules exist in many shapes, structures, and forms.

The physical, biochemical, and aromatic properties of Sesquiterpene molecules are unique because they are larger molecules than Monoterpenes. Since Sesquiterpene molecules are larger and heavier than Monoterpene molecules, they have a tendency to remain in the liquid essential oil, evaporate very slowly from the skin, and move slowly in the air.

The Sesquiterpene molecules in frankincense essential oil are valuable and bioactive. Even though less than 10% of the frankincense molecules are Sesquiterpenes, they are highly prized for their biologically effects.

Frankincense Essential Oil Sesquiterpenes	Content %
alpha-cubebene	0.1%
alpha-ylangene	0.1%
alpha-copaene	0.7%
beta-elemene	1.2%
trans-beta-caryophyllene	2.6%
beta-guaiene	0.1%
alpha-humulene	0.6%
allo-aromadendrene	0.2%
gamma-muurolene	0.4%
germacrene D	0.5%
alpha-muurolene	0.3%
alpha-selinene	0.4%
delta-cadinene	1.4%
Total	**8.7%**

Sesquiterpenes are considered the biological treasure chest of essential oils. Sesquiterpene molecules are small enough to cross the blood-brain barrier (as are Monoterpenes and Oxygenated Monoterpenes). Sesquiterpenes have been linked with many health benefits for the respiratory, cardiovascular, immune, nervous, and digestive systems.

The aroma of Sesquiterpene molecules is a function of their 3-dimensional shape, just like with Monoterpene molecules. The olfactory nerve endings tend to recognize only a limited portion of these larger molecules. As a result, the aroma of most Sesquiterpene molecules is similarly described as "woody", "earthy", and "spicy". Therefore, in contrast with Monoterpene molecules, most Sesquiterpene molecules have similar aromas.

- *beta*-caryophyllene = "spicy, peppery, woody"
- *alpha*-copaene = "woody, spicy, honey"
- *alpha*-gurjunene = "woody, balsamic"
- germacrene B = "woody, earthy, spicy"
- *beta*-farnesene = "woody, citrus, sweet"
- *delta*-cadinene = "fresh, woody, herbal"
- *alpha*-cedrene = "woody, cedar, sweet"

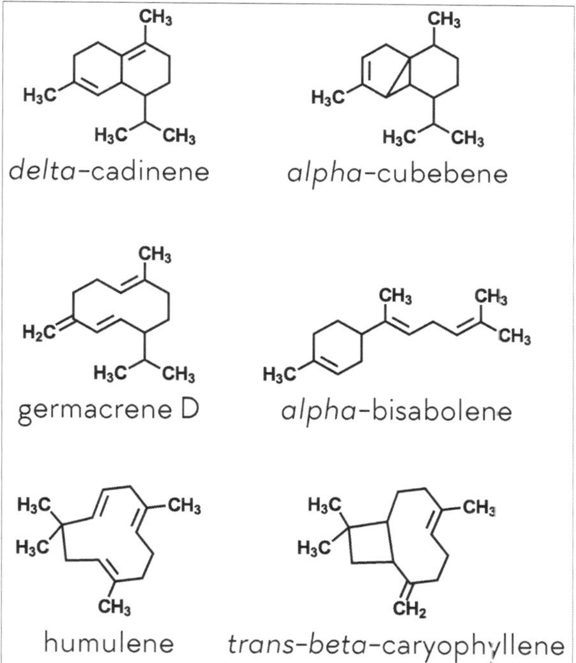

Figure 29. Biochemical structures of Sesquiterpene molecules.

Sesquiterpene molecules are known to have a **grounding effect** on the body, mind, and emotions. These healthful effects demonstrate the great importance of Sesquiterpene-rich essential oils.

Some examples of Sesquiterpene-rich essential oils are: yarrow, cedarwood, juniper, frankincense, myrrh, German chamomile, melissa (lemon balm), valerian, vitex, black pepper, ylang ylang, patchouli, ginger, and goldenrod.

OXYGENATED SESQUITERPENES

Oxygenated Sesquiterpenes are valuable molecules in essential oil. Oxygenated Sesquiterpenes contain 1, 2, or 3 extra Oxygen atoms added to the 15-Carbon Sesquiterpene molecule. The most common Oxygenated Sesquiterpenes contain one Oxygen atom, like Sesquiterpene Alcohols (C-O-H), Sesquiterpene Aldehydes (-HC=O), Sesquiterpene Ketones (>C=O), Sesquiterpene Ethers (C-O-C), and Sesquiterpene Oxides (C-O-C triangle).

The Oxygenated Sesquiterpenes in frankincense essential oil provide some of the longest lasting aromas. About 90 minutes after applying frankincense essential oil to your skin you can smell the heavenly "frankincense" aroma of Oxygenated Sesquiterpenes. The long-lasting aroma of Sesquiterpenes and Oxygenated Sesquiterpenes in frankincense may put you in a calm, meditative mood.

Frankincense Essential Oil Oxygenated Sesquiterpenes	Content %
spathulenol	0.1%
caryophyllene oxide	0.4%
viridiflorol	0.1%
gamma-eudesmol	0.3%
tau-cadinol	0.4%
beta-eudesmol	0.1%
Total	**1.4%**

Oxygenated Sesquiterpenes are not often discussed. They are difficult to find, yet their aroma is deep and long-lasting. They are large, heavy molecules. The scientists who separate and identify essential oil molecules using the **Gas Chromatograph-Mass Spectrometer (GC-MS)** instrument often overlook these Oxygenated Sesquiterpene molecules.

Less than one drop of essential oil is injected into the **gas chromatograph (GC)** portion of the GC-MS instrument where the essential oil molecules are gradually exposed to increasingly higher temperatures (usually starting at 40°C). While the molecules in the GC-MS instrument are heated up, the Monoterpene molecules are the first to move through the GC instrument, followed by the Oxygenated Monoterpenes, then the Sesquiterpenes, and finally the Oxygenated Sesquiterpenes. The GC portion of the instrument can separate all 100-300 molecules in the essential oil in less than one hour.

The **mass spectrometer (MS)** portion of the instrument blasts each molecule into fragments as it exits the gas chromatograph. The blast is like a hammer shattering a ceramic vase. Each molecule produces a consistent fragment pattern that is distinct from other molecules. The mass spectrometer uses the fragment pattern to identify the molecules. The mass spectrometer uses an extensive **Digital MS Library of Standard Molecules** containing over 500,000 molecule fragment patterns to identify and name the separated molecules.

The problem is that there are very few Oxygenated Sesquiterpene fragment patterns in the mass spectrometer digital library. Therefore, scientists have a difficult time identifying and naming these larger molecules.

Oxygenated Sesquiterpene Alcohols. Sesquiterpene Alcohols have a broad range of aromas such as "woody, floral, spicy, and sweet". Some Sesquiterpene Alcohols occur in only a few plant species and have very distinctive aromas. For instance, cedrenol and cedrol = "cedarwood aroma" are commonly found in cedarwood and juniper essential oils. Similarly, *alpha*-santalol

= "sandalwood aroma" is found in high abundance in sandalwood oil, and patchoulol = "patchouli aroma" is characteristic of patchouli essential oil.

- *beta*-bisabolol = "floral, peppery, green"
- *beta*-cubenol = "spicy, herbal, tea"
- *alpha*-elemol = "green, woody, sweet"
- nerolidol = "floral, green, citrus"
- *tau*-muurolol = "herbal, spicy, honey"
- viridiflorol = "sweet, green, herbal"
- spathulenol = "earthy, herbal, fruity"
- *alpha*-santalol = "woody, sandalwood"
- guaiol = "guaiacwood, rose, woody"
- patchoulol = "patchouli, earthy, camphoreous"
- cedrol = "cedarwood, woody, dry"

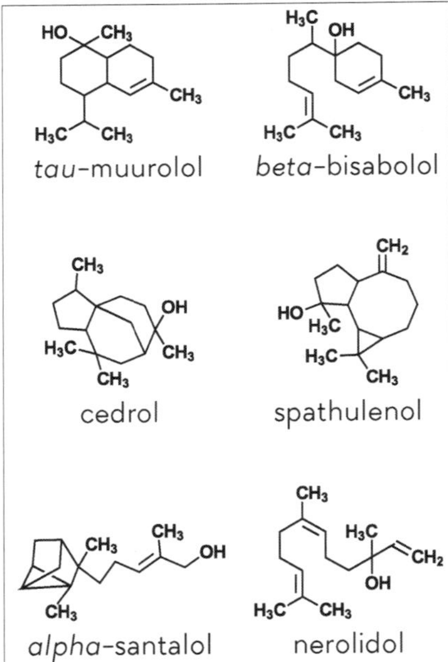

Figure 30. Biochemical structures of Oxygenated Sesquiterpene Alcohol molecules.

Oxygenated Sesquiterpene Aldehydes. There are few Sesquiterpene Aldehyde molecules. The most common Sesquiterpene Aldehydes are *alpha*-sinensal and *beta*-sinensal found in small percentages in cold-pressed citrus oils. The aroma intensity of these two molecules is quite intense. The overall aroma of the sinensal molecules is "citrus, orange, sweet".

- *alpha*-sinensal (citrus) = "citrus, orange, mandarin"
- *beta*-sinensal (citrus) = "orange, sweet, fresh"
- E,Z-farnesal = "floral, minty"

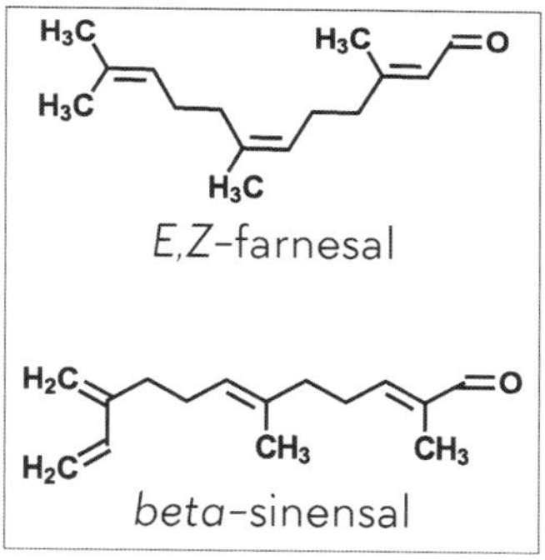

E,Z-farnesal

beta-sinensal

Figure 31. Biochemical structures of Oxygenated Sesquiterpene Aldehyde molecules.

Oxygenated Sesquiterpene Ketones. Sesquiterpene Ketones are somewhat common. The aroma of Sesquiterpene Ketones is invariably associated with the typical aroma of the plant species. Nootkatone is the key aroma indicator of grapefruit essential oil, while zingerone is a key aroma in ginger essential oil. Plants do not need to produce Sesquiterpene Ketones in high quantities because the aroma intensity of these molecules is extremely high. The general aroma of Sesquiterpene Ketone molecules can be described as "woody, spicy, and warm".

- zingerone (ginger) = "ginger, spicy, balsamic"
- *alpha*-vetivone (vetiver) = "warm, pleasant, powerful"

- khusimone (vetiver) = "vetiver, woody"
- nootkatone (grapefruit) = "grapefruit, citrus, orange"
- *alpha*-alantone (cedarwood) = "cedarwood, woody"
- deodarone (cedarwood) = "cedarwood, woody"
- *alpha*-ionone (cedarwood) = "sweet, woody, floral"

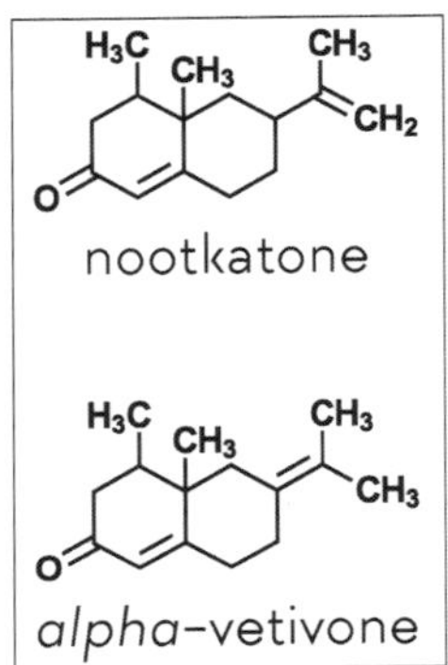

Figure 32. Biochemical structures of Oxygenated Sesquiterpene Ketone molecules.

Oxygenated Sesquiterpene Ethers and Oxides. There are just a few examples of Sesquiterpene Ethers and Oxides. Little is known about their aroma profiles. German chamomile and Roman chamomile contain bisabolol oxide A and bisabolol oxide B molecules. The Sesquiterpene Oxide molecule caryophyllene oxide is found in frankincense and carrot seed essential oils.

- chrysamthemyl oxide = "green, floral, chrysanthemum"
- bisabolol oxide A = "floral, peppery, clean"
- caryophyllene oxide = "sweet, woody, carrot"

Oxygenated Sesquiterpenes love Moist Surfaces. Oxygenated Sesquiterpenes love moist surfaces inside your body; namely the lungs, sinuses, skin, blood, tissues and organs. This relationship takes place because the Oxygen portion of the Sesquiterpene molecule has a strong affinity for water molecules (H_2O) and moist surfaces.

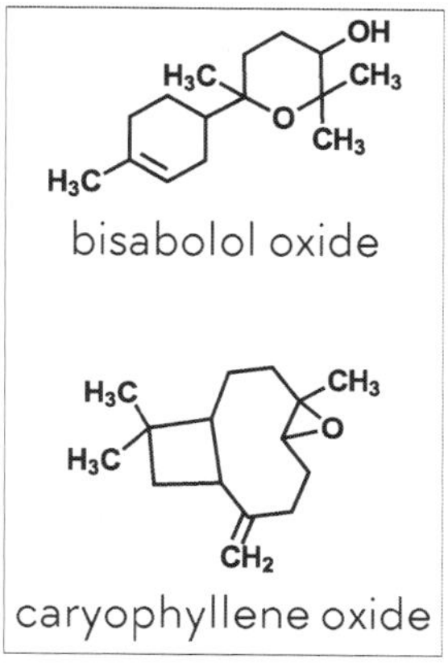

Figure 33. Biochemical structures of Oxygenated Sesquiterpene Ether and Oxide molecules.

Some of the great biological and emotional benefits of Oxygenated Sesquiterpenes can be credited to their endurance. These heavy molecules that affix themselves to moist surfaces endure for long hours, numerous day, and even weeks. While they remain inside the body, they are given opportunities to "act". Oxygenated Sesquiterpenes are very persistent.

TRY OXYGENATED SESQUITERPENES

Essential oils that contain Oxygenated Sesquiterpenes include blue cypress, Taiwan red hinoki (hong kuai), ylang ylang, sandalwood, myrrh, ledum, German chamomile, grapefruit, ginger, patchouli, and vetiver.

Try inhaling the invisible vapors of Oxygenated Sesquiterpene-rich essential oils. Take five deep breaths to fill your lungs with

Oxygenated Sesquiterpenes. You will likely experience powerful changes to your emotional feelings, mental state, and physical condition. You will find that the aroma of the Oxygenated Sesquiterpenes can be detected in your breath for hours. Place a drop of cedarwood essential oil on the leather of your wallet or purse; the Oxygenated Sesquiterpene aroma will persist for days. Place a drop or two of sandalwood or myrrh oil on a piece of wood or wooden furniture and the aroma will last for days.

EXPLORING SUMMARY

- Sesquiterpene molecules contain 15 Carbon atoms and a number of Hydrogen atoms.
- The aroma of most Sesquiterpene molecules tend to be described as "woody", "earthy", and "spicy".
- Sesquiterpenes contain 1, 2, or 3 Oxygen atoms added to the 15-Carbon Sesquiterpene molecule.
- Sesquiterpene Alcohol molecules tend to have a "woody, floral, spicy, sweet" aroma.
- Sesquiterpene Aldehyde molecules tend to have a "citrus, orange, sweet" aroma.
- Sesquiterpene Ketone molecules tend to have a "woody, spicy, warm" aroma.
- Some of the great biological and emotional benefits of Oxygenated Sesquiterpenes can be credited to their endurance on wet or dry surfaces.
- Oxygenated Sesquiterpenes love moist surfaces inside your body – the lungs, sinuses, skin, blood, tissues and organs.

GLOSSARY

Sesquiterpene (SES-kwi-tur-pēn): A 15-Carbon essential oil hydrocarbon molecule formed by connecting 1 ½ terpene units (3 isoprene units). "Sesqui-" means "one and a half" and "-terpene" means "10-Carbon molecule".

Oxygenated Sesquiterpene: A 15-Carbon essential oil molecule possessing an Oxygen atom.

Grounding Effect: Placing the body and mind in a state of confidence, trust, and feeling close to nature.

Gas Chromatograph-Mass Spectrometer (GC-MS): is an analytical instrument for separating and identifying hundreds of molecules present in essential oils.

Gas chromatograph (GC): Gas Chromatograph is an analytical testing instrument for separating hundreds of molecules in essential oils. The molecules are separated by exposing them to increasingly higher temperatures from 40°C to 270°C.

Mass Spectrometer (MS): Mass Spectrometer is an analytical testing instrument for identifying essential oil molecules separated by the GC instrument.

Digital MS Library of Standard Molecules: An extensive digital library of molecule fragment patterns for over 500,000 different standard molecules. The GC-MS software searches the digital MS library to find a match to the molecules in the essential oil being tested. The digital library provides best-suggested matches and the chemical name for each match.

Oxygenated Sesquiterpene Alcohol: A 15-Carbon essential oil molecule containing one Oxygen atom sandwiched between a Carbon atom and a Hydrogen atom anywhere in the molecule (C-O-H).

Oxygenated Sesquiterpene Aldehyde: A 15-Carbon essential oil molecule containing one Oxygen atom is connected to a Carbon atom with a double bond at a terminal end of the molecule (-HC=0).

Oxygenated Sesquiterpene Ketone: A 15-Carbon essential oil molecule containing one Oxygen atom is connected to a Carbon atom with a double bond within the middle of the molecule (>C=0).

Oxygenated Sesquiterpene Ether: A 15-Carbon essential oil molecule containing one Oxygen atom sandwiched between two Carbon atom chains in the middle of the molecule (C-O-C).

Oxygenated Sesquiterpene Oxide: A 15-Carbon essential oil molecule containing one Oxygen atom connected to two adjacent Carbon atoms to form a triangular shape in the molecule.

DR. WOOLLEY'S CHALLENGE

- Copy one molecule shape from each group: Sesquiterpene, Sesquiterpene Alcohol, Sesquiterpene Aldehyde, Sesquiterpene Ketone, Sesquiterpene Ether, and Sesquiterpene Oxide.
- Explain to a child or adult how the properties of Sesquiterpenes differ from those of Monoterpenes.
- Explain to a child or adult why the aroma of most Sesquiterpene molecules is described as "woody", "earthy", and "spicy".
- Write a short paragraph describing the interaction between Oxygenated Sesquiterpenes and moist surfaces.
- Go on-line and search for a photo and description of a gas chromatograph-mass spectrometer (GC-MS) instrument. Describe the functions of the GC and the MS portions of the instrument. Describe the functions of the digital mass spectra library of standard molecules.

9

Diterpene Molecules

DITERPENES

There are 20 Carbon atoms and numerous Hydrogen atoms in the basic formula of Diterpene molecules. "Di-" means "two" and "-terpene" means "10-Carbon molecule". They can be referred to as hydrocarbons because they contain only Carbon and Hydrogen atoms. Diterpene molecules are larger than Sesquiterpene molecules. They are less soluble (mixable) in water than Sesquiterpenes and Monoterpenes. Diterpene molecules remain on the skin long after the Monoterpenes and Sesquiterpenes have evaporated.

There is only one observed Diterpene molecule (cembrene) in *Boswellia carterii* frankincense essential oil from Somalia. In contrast, there are numerous Diterpene molecules in the hydro-distilled essential oil of *Boswellia sacra* frankincense from Oman.

Frankincense Essential Oil Diterpenes	Content %
cembrene	0.1%
Total	**0.1%**

Plants produce Diterpene molecules in their essential oil-filled secretory cells, but they are sometimes not observed in the distilled essential oil. There are two reasons for the lack of finding Diterpene, Oxygenated Diterpene, Triterpene, and Oxygenated Triterpene molecules in the distilled essential oils; the upper temperature limit of distillation and the maximum temperature limit of GC-MS analysis.

STEAM DISTILLATION AND ITS TEMPERATURE LIMITATIONS

The temperature that water boils, 212°F (100°C), is the highest temperature of Steam Distillation and Hydro-distillation. Since Steam Distillation usually takes place near atmospheric pressure (low pressure), then 212°F (100°C) is the **upper temperature limit of distillation**. Essential oil molecules that easily, moderately, and slowly evaporate (molecules that transform from a liquid into a vapor) at 212°F (100°C) are the ones that end up collected in the final condensed essential oil.

The "easily evaporated" molecules (Monoterpenes and Oxygenated Monoterpenes) will achieve a distillation transfer rate from plant-to-essential oil of close to 100%. This means that nearly all of these molecules will leave the plant material and show up in the essential oil.

The "moderately evaporated" molecules (Sesquiterpenes and Oxygenated Sesquiterpenes) roughly transfer about 30-70% of molecules from plant material to essential oil in the distillation process. If you smell the distilled residue plant material, you may be able to detect the aroma of Sesquiterpene and Oxygenated Sesquiterpene molecules.

Most of the "slowly evaporated" molecules (Diterpenes and Oxygenated Diterpenes) do not receive enough energy to transition from liquid form to vapor form at the 212°F (100°C). Instead, these "slowly evaporated" molecules prefer to remain as liquids in the plant material. Only 1-5% of the larger Diterpenes and Oxygenated Diterpenes that are in plant material make it into the collected essential oil. Diterpene molecules are near the upper temperature limit of Steam Distillation and Hydro-distillation. The distilled residue plant material still possesses most of the Diterpene and Oxygenated Diterpene molecules.

The "reluctantly evaporated" molecules (Triterpenes, and Oxygenated Triterpenes) do not tend to vaporize at the 212°F (100°C). At the upper temperature limit of distillation, less than 1% of Triterpenes and Oxygenated Triterpenes move from the plant material to the condensed essential oil.

The "stationary" molecules (Tetraterpenes and Oxygenated Tetraterpenes) do not evaporate at the upper temperature limit of distillation. Steam temperatures are not high enough to energize the Tetraterpene molecules from the plant material into the essential oil. Tetraterpenes are colorful molecules that are retained in distilled plant material.

GC-MS AND ITS TEMPERATURE LIMITATIONS

The second reason Diterpenes, Oxygenated Diterpenes, Triterpenes, and Oxygenated Triterpenes are infrequently observed in distilled essential oils is the **maximum temperature limit of GC-MS analysis**. A typical **GC-MS temperature program** operates from between 40°C up to 260°C. The molecules of essential oil injected into the GC-MS are separated in the **GC-MS capillary column** that is situated in the GC-MS oven. The essential oil molecules are separated by slowly increasing the temperature in the GC-MS oven. Each capillary column has a designated **capillary column maximum temperature limit**.

In the GC-MS instrument, the Monoterpene and Oxygenated Monoterpene molecules separate at around 80-180°C; and the Sesquiterpene and Oxygenated Sesquiterpene molecules separate at about 180-250°C. However, the Diterpene and Oxygenated Diterpene molecules require temperatures of 250-300°C, and the Triterpene and Oxygenated Triterpene molecules can only be separated at 300-350°C. Therefore, since most GC-MS analyses are operated only to 260°C they detect only some of the Diterpene and Oxygenated Diterpenes; and none of the Triterpene and Oxygenated Triterpene molecules.

FUSED RINGS OF DITERPENE MOLECULES

Diterpene molecules typically possess connected or **fused ring structures** of 6-Carbon atoms. The molecules have a honeycomb-like appearance. These Diterpene molecules possess three fused rings of Carbon atoms. Below are some examples of common Diterpenes and their plant sources.

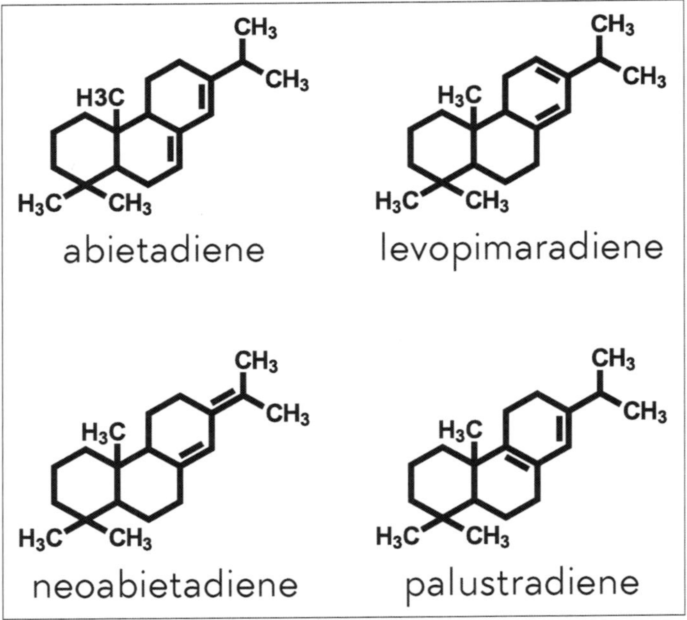

Figure 34. Biochemical structures of Diterpene molecules.

Conifer species – abietane, strobane, kaurane, atisarane, pimarane, palustrane

Pinus species (Pine) – cembrene, abietadiene, neoabietadiene, levopiramadiene, palustradiene

Picea species (Spruce)–abietadiene, neoabietadiene, levopiramadiene, palustradiene, piramadiene,

Abies species (Fir) – abietadiene, sandaracopimaradiene, dehydroabietadiene, *ent*-kaurene

Boswellia species (Frankincense) – cembrene

Cinnamomum camphora (White Camphor) – camphorene, hishorene

OXYGENATED DITERPENES

As essential oil molecules get larger, they tend to be more oxygenated. They typically occur as Diterpene Alcohols, Diterpene Aldehydes, and Diterpene Carboxylic Acids. These **Oxygenated Diterpenes** may exist in relatively high concentrations (10-40%) in the essential oil stored in trichomes, secretory sacs and resin canals, but only a small percentage of these "slightly evaporated" molecules are transferred to the condensed essential oil during the Steam Distillation process.

Frankincense essential oil contains several Oxygenated Diterpene molecules. Research has shown that incensol and incensyl acetate molecules are unique to frankincense essential oils.

Frankincense Essential Oil Oxygenated Diterpenes	Content %
cembrenol	0.1%
incensol	0.4%
incensyl acetate	0.1%
Total	**0.6%**

There is a greater assortment of aromas with the addition of an Oxygen atom to Diterpene molecules. Oxygenated Diterpenes have very long-lasting aroma, but the intensity is very low. This low intensity is due to the fact that these molecules slowly escape the surface to mix with the air. They tend to remain on the surface after they are applied. Here are some examples of Oxygenated Diterpenes and their typical aromas.

- abienol = "woody, amber, ambergris"
- sclareol = "sweet, balsamic, sage"
- phytol = "floral, balsamic, powdery"
- isophytol = "floral, herbal, green"
- geranyl linalool = "floral, rose, balsamic"

Plant DNA performs all the biochemical transformations of Diterpenes into Oxygenated Diterpenes. In general, Diterpene molecules are first converted into Diterpene Alcohols, which in turn can be converted into Diterpene Aldehydes, which in turn can be converted into Diterpene Carboxylic Acids. An example of this **biochemical conversion** is depicted with the Diterpene and Oxygenated Diterpene molecules of fir trees. Abietadiene is converted into abietadienol (-COH), which is converted to abietadienal (-HC=O), which is converted into abietic acid (-CO_2H).

There is not much to say regarding the aroma since so little aroma research has been performed for Diterpenes. The fact that the Diterpene Alcohol abienol is described as "woody, amber, ambergris" and sclareol's aroma as "sweet, balsamic, sage" gives us an idea what the aromas of other Oxygenated Diterpene molecules may add to essential oils.

Scientists have only identified a small number of Oxygenated Diterpene molecules in essential oils. They are commonly found in essential oils of pine, spruce, fir, juniper, and cypress trees. In addition, they are found in other essential oils like cistus, frankincense, jasmine and clary sage. However, scientists typically fail

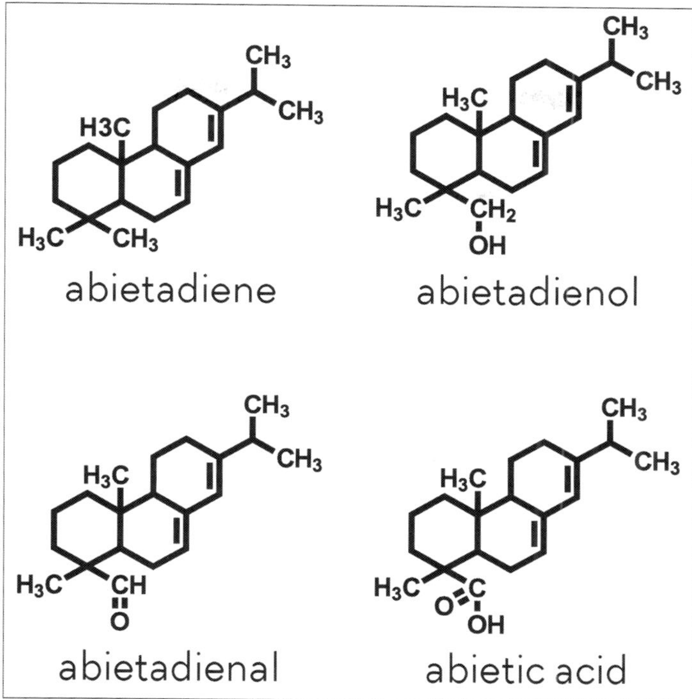

Figure 35. Biochemical structures depicting the natural conversion from Diterpene to Oxygenated Diterpene Alcohol, Aldehyde, and Carboxylic acid molecules.

to observe Oxygenated Diterpenes because they do not operate their GC-MS to the required temperatures (250-300°C) and these molecules may not be identifiable because they are not found in the Digital MS Library of Standard Molecules.

Conifer species (Pine, Spruce, Fir) – abietadienol, neoabietadienol, levopimaradienol

Conifer species (Pine, Spruce, Fir) – abietadienal, isopimaradienal, palustradienal

Conifer species (Pine, Spruce, Fir) – abietic acid, pimaric acid, sandaracopimaric acid

Juniperus phoenicia (Juniper) – pimaric acid, *epi*-abietol, sandaracopimaric acid,

Cupressus sempervirens (Cypress) – abienol, manool, sempervirol, totarol,

Vitex agnus-castus (Chaste tree)–chastol and *epi*-chastol

Cistus ladanifer (Cistus) – labdanenol, labdanendiol

Boswellia species (Frankincense) – incensol, manool,

Jasminum officianale (Jasmine) – phytol

Salvia sclarea (Clary Sage)–sclareol

EXPLORING SUMMARY

- The largest molecules in steam distilled and hydro-distilled essential oils are typically 20-Carbon Diterpenes and Oxygenated Diterpenes.
- Diterpenes are commonly separated and identified by GC-MS analytical instruments.
- The aroma of Diterpene molecules is not easily distinguished because these large molecules do not readily enter the air.

GLOSSARY

Diterpene: A 20-Carbon essential oil molecule formed by connecting 2 terpene units. "Di-" means "two" and "-terpene" means "10-Carbon molecule".

Upper temperature limit of distillation: Diterpene and Oxygenated Diterpene molecules are typically the largest essential oil molecules collected from Steam Distillation and Hydrodistillation.

Maximum temperature limit of GC-MS analysis: The highest temperature that the GC oven is programmed for. The Capillary Column Upper Temperature Limit is the Maximum Temperature Limit of GC-MS Analysis.

GC-MS temperature program: The oven heating program that typically runs between 40°C up to 260°C.

GC-MS capillary column: A long, flexible fiber optic tube situated within the GC-MS oven where the essential oil molecules are separated. A thin film of silicone polymer is bonded to the inner surface of the tube in order to affect the separation of molecules.

Capillary column maximum temperature limit: Each fused silica capillary column has a maximum operating temperature. The maximum GC-MS oven temperature needs to be kept at or below the maximum column temperature.

Fused ring structure: When 6-Carbon rings are connected side-by-side in a honeycomb-like pattern.

Oxygenated Diterpene: A 20-Carbon Diterpene molecule containing 1 or more Oxygen atoms to form Diterpene Alcohols, Diterpene Ketones, Diterpene Aldehydes and Diterpene Carboxylic acids.

Biochemical conversion: A process where plant enzymes and ATP biochemical energy molecules are used to convert an essential oil molecule into a slightly different molecule.

DR. WOOLLEY'S CHALLENGE

- Explain to a child or adult why Diterpenes are the largest molecules typically found in steam distilled and hydro-distilled essential oils.
- Copy two chemical structures of Diterpene and two chemical structures of Oxygenated Diterpene molecules. Write down their chemical names.

10

Triterpene Molecules

TRITERPENES AND OXYGENATED TRITERPENES

These large 30-Carbon molecules (6 isoprenes) form a class of very bioactive essential oil components. "Tri-" means "three" and "-terpene" means "10-Carbon molecule". **Triterpenes** are hydrocarbons and **water insoluble**, meaning they do not readily mix with water. **Oxygenated Triterpenes** are slightly **water soluble** because they contain Oxygen atoms. Triterpene and Oxygenated Triterpene molecules are the largest aromatic molecules that plants produce. Triterpenes and Oxygenated Triterpenes are present in essential oils stored in trichomes, secretory sacs, and resin canals of plants and trees.

Triterpene and Oxygenated Triterpene molecules have been found in abundance in frankincense oleogum-resins. Unfortunately, the upper temperature limit of distillation prevents Triterpenes and Oxygenated Triterpenes from being transferred in abundance into distilled essential oils.

Triterpenes also possess fused rings of 6-Carbon atoms giving them a honeycomb appearance. Triterpene molecules are hydrocarbons that are constructed solely of Carbon and

Hydrogen atoms. Triterpenes are transported within the resin canals of frankincense trees by the smaller Monoterpene and Sesquiterpene molecules.

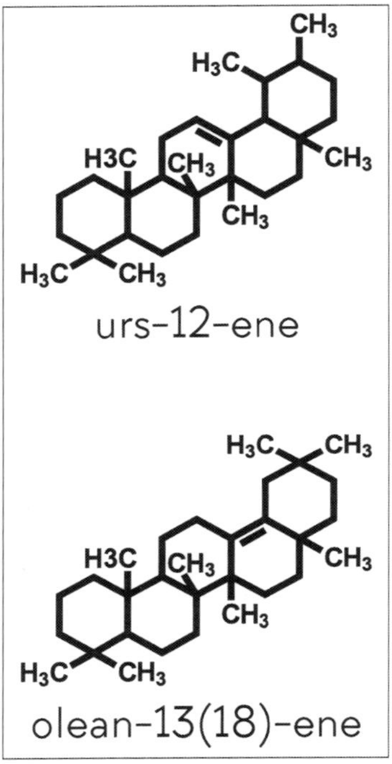

Figure 36. Biochemical structures of Triterpene molecules.

Extracting Triterpenes and Oxygenated Triterpenes

These large Triterpene and Oxygenated Triterpene molecules show up when the plant material is extracted with chemical solvents (e.g., hexane, ethanol, or ethyl acetate). **Chemical solvent extraction** is very effective and efficient. The Triterpene extract is usually concentrated by evaporating off the volatile chemical solvents.

Another method for extracting Triterpenes and Oxygenated Triterpenes is using **Supercritical Fluid Extraction (SFE)** with Carbon Dioxide (CO_2) as the extraction fluid. In SFE, the essential oil is extracted at low temperatures and high pressures.

Supercritical Carbon Dioxide extraction favors the larger molecules of Sesquiterpenes, Diterpenes and Triterpenes.

This chapter includes examples of some Triterpene and Oxygenated Triterpenes that were identified from chemical solvent extracts and Supercritical Fluid extracts. These Triterpenes do not have much of an odor because the molecules reluctantly evaporate from the liquid extract.

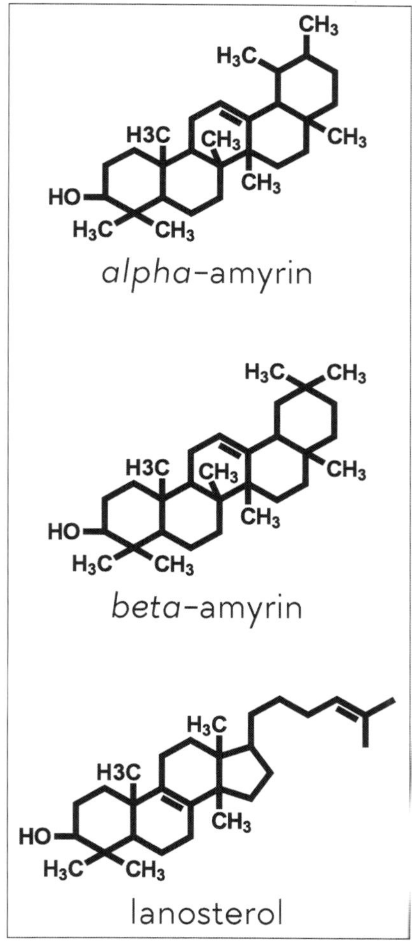

Figure 37. Biochemical structures of Oxygenated Triterpene Alcohol molecules.

Analyzing Triterpenes and Oxygenated Triterpenes

There are two analytical methods used to detect these large Triterpene and Oxygenated Triterpene molecules in essential oils. The first method is called **High Temperature GC-MS** in which the oven temperature of the gas chromatograph is taken as high as 300°C to 340°C. High temperature GC-MS requires a capillary column that has a maximum temperature limit of at least 340°C. I prefer to use the High Temperature GC-MS method for analyzing Triterpenes and Oxygenated Triterpenes because the mass spectrometer can help identify the molecules.

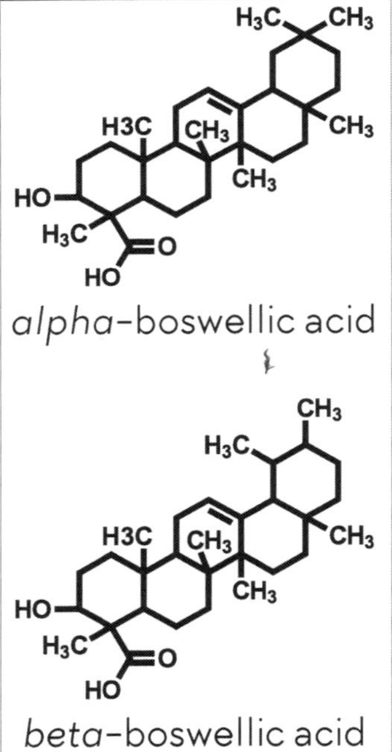

Figure 38. Biochemical structures of Oxygenated Triterpene Carboxylic acid molecules.

The second method is called **High Performance Liquid Chromatography (HPLC)**. In HPLC, water and chemical solvents are used to separate the Oxygenated Triterpene Carboxylic acid molecules. In fact, HPLC separations of *Boswellia carterii* frankincense and *Boswellia sacra* frankincense essential oils have proven the presence of 1-2% Triterpene boswellic acids. Considering that frankincense contains 20-25% boswellic acids by weight in their oleogum-resin shows the prevalence of Oxygenated Triterpene molecules.

Triterpene and Oxygenated Triterpene molecules are abundant in frankincense oleogum-resins. The molecules of urs-12-ene and olean-13(18)-ene provide a framework for the Oxygenated Triterpene molecules. Urs-12-ene forms the basis for *alpha*-amyrin and *beta*-boswellic acid. Olean-13(18)-ene is the base molecule that transforms to *beta*-amyrin and *alpha*-boswellic acid. All these molecular conversions are dictated by the DNA instructions housed within the cells of frankincense trees.

Triterpene and Oxygenated Triterpenes have been found in various frankincense oleogum-resins and in some plant extracts. These large Triterpene and Oxygenated Triterpene molecules have been identified by High Temperature GC-MS and analytical HPLC.

Boswellia sacra (Sacra frankincense) – urs-12-ene and olean-13(18)-ene

Boswellia sacra (Sacra frankincense) – *alpha*-amyrin, *beta*-amyrin, and lanosterol,

Boswellia sacra (Sacra frankincense) – *alpha*-boswellic acid and *beta*-boswellic acid

Boswellia carterii (Carterii frankincense) – urs-12-ene and olean-13(18)-ene,

Boswellia carterii (Carterii frankincense) – *alpha*-amyrin, *beta*-amyrin, and lanosterol,

Boswellia carterii (Carterii frankincense) – *alpha*-boswellic acid and *beta*-boswellic acid

Boswellia frereana (Frereana frankincense) – *alpha*-amyrin and *beta*-amyrin,

Boswellia frereana (Frereana frankincense) – lupeol, *epi*-lupeol, and lupeol acetate

Chrysanthemum indicum (Chrysanthenum) – *alpha*-amyrin and *beta*-amyrin,

Chrysanthemum indicum (Chrysanthenum) – lupeol, sitosterol, and taraxasterol

Melissa officinalis (Melissa) – germanicol

Jasminum officinale (Jasmine) – squalene

Oxygenated Triterpenes are being wildly heralded for their anti-inflammatory properties. The healing benefits of the Triterpene alcohols sitosterol and lanosterol are well documented. The acclaimed anti-inflammatory and anti-cancer properties of *alpha*-amyrin, *beta*-amyrin, lanosterol, and the boswellic acids in frankincense oleogum-resins is of great interest to health and medical fields. New medical research on *Boswellia frereana* frankincense has pointed to the anticipated anti-inflammatory and anti-cancer benefits of the Oxygenated Triterpene molecules lupeol, *epi*-lupeol, and lupeol acetate.

EXPLORING SUMMARY

- Triterpenes are produced and stored by plants in trichomes, secretory sacs, and resin canals, but are seldom found in distilled essential oils.
- The 30-Carbon Triterpene and Oxygenated Triterpene molecules are not sufficiently energized during Steam Distillation or Hydro-distillation to be collected in the essential oil.
- Triterpenes are highly bioactive in the body. Published research has shown Triterpene molecules have anti-inflammatory and anti-cancer properties.

GLOSSARY

Triterpene: A 30-Carbon essential oil molecule formed by connecting 3 terpenes units. "Tri-" means "three" and "-terpene" means "10-Carbon molecule".

Water Insoluble: Describing when a molecule does not completely mix in water (e.g. most essential oil molecules are insoluble in water because they separate from water).

Oxygenated Triterpene: A 30-Carbon Triterpene molecule that contains at least one Oxygen atom.

Water Soluble: Describing when a molecule mixes with water. Some molecules are slightly water soluble, while other molecules are completely water soluble.

Chemical solvent extraction: A method for extracting essential oil molecules from plant material by using chemical solvents (e.g., hexane, ethanol). Chemical solvents can extract molecules ranging in size from Monoterpenes to Tetraterpenes.

Supercritical Fluid Extraction (SFE): A high pressure and low temperature extraction method that creates a fluid to extract large molecules from plant material. SFE is a "green technology" because it does not use chemical solvents, just renewable Carbon Dioxide gas.

High Temperature GC-MS: An analytical GC-MS instrument equipped with a capillary column that has an upper temperature limit ranging from 300°C to 340°C.

High Performance Liquid Chromatography (HPLC): An analytical separation instrument that uses water and chemical solvents to separate large molecules like Triterpenes and Tetraterpenes.

DR. WOOLLEY'S CHALLENGE

- Copy two chemical structures of Triterpene molecules and two chemical structures of Oxygenated Triterpene molecules. Write down their chemical names.
- Write a paragraph discussing why large Triterpene molecules are not typically found in steam distilled and hydro-distilled essential oils.
- Explain to a child or adult why Triterpene and Tetraterpene molecules are not known for their aromas.

11

Tetraterpene Molecules

TETRATERPENES AND OXYGENATED TETRATERPENES

Tetraterpenes are very large 40-Carbon molecules and are also known as **Carotenes**. "Tetra-"means "four" and "-terpene" means "10-Carbon molecule". **Oxygenated Tetraterpenes** are 40-Carbon molecules that contain at least one Oxygen atom. Oxygenated Tetraterpenes are also known as **Carotenoids**.

There are over 500 known Tetraterpene and Oxygenated Tetraterpene molecules found in nature. A wide variety of them are found in colorful fruits and vegetables, including citrus fruits. Interestingly, these large molecules are not known for their aromas. Instead, Tetraterpene and Oxygenated Tetraterpene molecules are known for their natural colors. They display colors such as yellow, orange, red, green, blue, and purple. They are also referred to as **pigments** or color molecules. The color changes of ripening citrus fruits are a display of the changing concentration of Tetraterpene and Oxygenated Tetraterpene molecules in the peel.

Citrus trees use these Tetraterpene and Oxygenated Tetraterpene color pigments as indicators of fruit maturation and as color patterns in citrus petals to attract pollinating birds and insects. The changing color of maturing citrus fruits on your countertop is a process where the types and concentrations of Carotenes and Carotenoids change over time. There are Tetraterpene and Oxygenated Tetraterpene molecules in most cold-pressed citrus oils. They are the molecules that add color.

You will NOT find Tetraterpene and Oxygenated Tetraterpene molecules in steam distilled and hydro-distilled essential oils, even though they are produced by the plant. At the upper temperature limit of distillation, 212°F (100°C), the only molecules collected are Monoterpenes, Oxygenated Monoterpenes, Sesquiterpenes, Oxygenated Sesquiterpenes, Diterpenes, Oxygenated Diterpenes and some Triterpenes. Tetraterpene and Oxygenated Tetraterpene molecules are even larger and are not readily energized by the heat of steam. These large 40-Carbon essential oil molecules remain in the distilled residue plant material that is bound for the compost pile.

The industrial cold-pressing methods that express essential oils from citrus peels collect all the molecules, from Monoterpenes to Tetraterpenes. Citrus essential oils are dominated (50-95%) by Monoterpene molecules, especially limonene. These essential oils contain a combined 1-2% of flavorful aldehyde molecules called octanal, nonanal, decanal, undecanal, and dodecanal. Citrus oils also contain about 5-40% Oxygenated Monoterpenes, 1-3% Sesquiterpenes, 1-3% Oxygenated Sesquiterpenes, 1-2% Coumarins and Furanocoumarins, and 1-2% Tetraterpenes. These molecules create the aroma, flavor, and colors of citrus essential oils.

CHEMISTRY OF TETRATERPENE AND OXYGENATED TETRATERPENE MOLECULES

Citrus essential oils contain some unique molecules called Coumarins, Furanocoumarins, Tetraterpenes, and Oxygenated Tetraterpenes. The Coumarins and Furanocoumarins are a special class of molecules that will be discussed in the next chapter.

Surprisingly, Tetraterpene and Oxygenated Tetraterpene molecules do not look like the honeycomb-shaped Diterpene and Triterpene molecules. Instead of the fused 6-Carbon rings of Diterpenes and Triterpenes, these 40-Carbon molecules are elongated with alternating double bonds (=) and single bonds (-). This alternating double bond and single bond pattern allows the Tetraterpene and Oxygenated Tetraterpene molecules to capture specific wavelengths of sunlight. The wavelengths they don't absorb are the colors we see. Their colorful properties have made them famous as natural pigments for dyed clothing, dyed wool for rug weaving, and as natural colorants in foods and beverages.

The structure of the Tetraterpene and Oxygenated Tetraterpene molecules determines the color we see. A slight structural change to one of these 40-Carbon molecules can create a different color. The yellow-orange color of *beta*-carotene and the yellow color of *alpha*-carotene is the result of switching the position of just one double bond in the nearly identical structures.

As citrus fruit ripens, it goes through a few color changes. During the cool springtime, the pollinated citrus blossoms turn into small developing green fruits. The fruits remain green-colored as they grow larger during the hot summer months. As days become shorter and nights become longer, the daily temperatures begin to drop. This triggers a color change from green to yellow. As the fruit nears its peak of sweetness, the citrus fruit takes on its final colors: yellow for lemons, yellow-orange for oranges, orange for mandarins, pink for grapefruits, and orange-red for tangerines. These color changes in the peel and pulp are a result of the DNA-controlled production of Tetraterpene and Oxygenated Tetraterpene molecules.

Color Molecules in Orange Oil

The diversity and concentration of Tetraterpene and Oxygenated Tetraterpene molecules produced and stored in endodermal secretory sacs in orange (*Citrus sinensis*) peels provide the color changes as the citrus fruit ripens. There may be 10-30

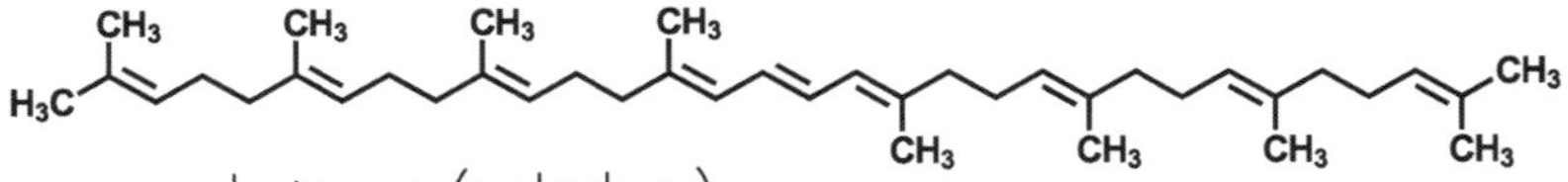

phytoene (colorless)

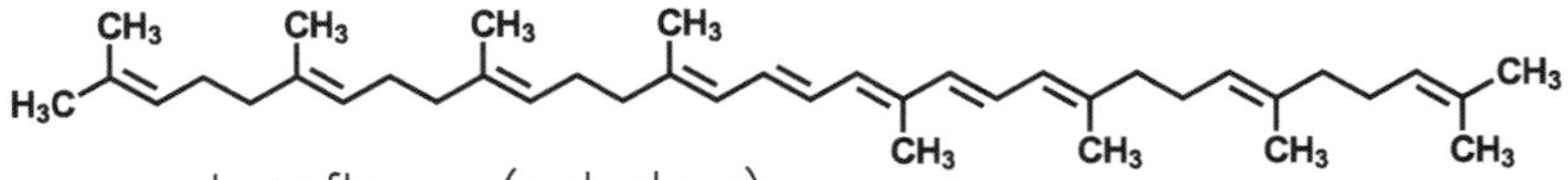

phytofluene (colorless)

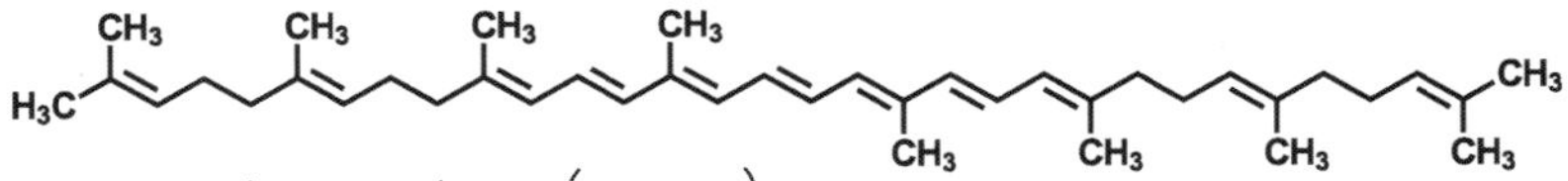

zeta-carotene (cream)

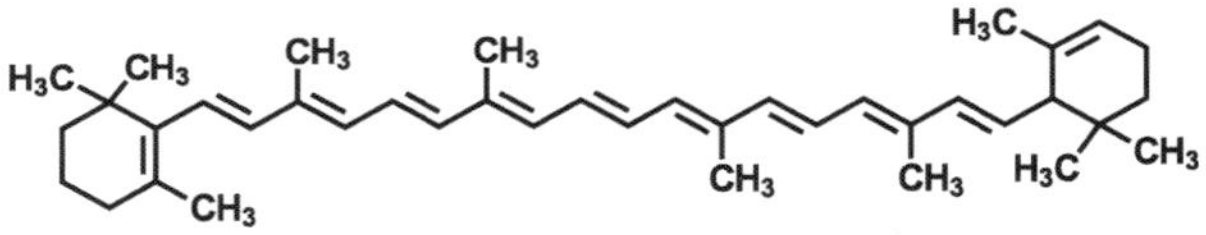

alpha-carotene (yellow)

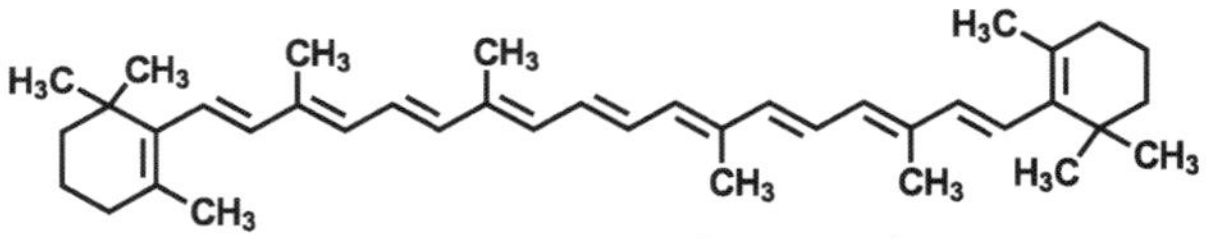

beta-carotene (orange)

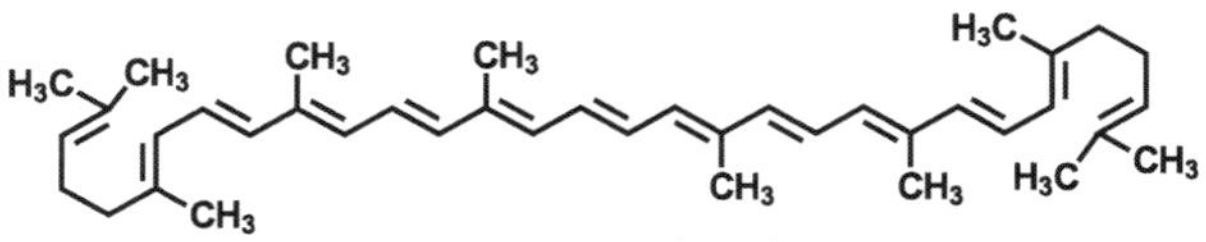

lycopene (red)

Figure 39. Biochemical structures of Tetraterpene pigment molecules.

Tetraterpenes and Oxygenated Tetraterpenes in the peel over the maturation time of citrus fruits.

As the orange fruit develops from the blossom it is green in color. The green color comes from the photosynthetic (non-Tetraterpenes) color pigments chlorophyll *a* (light green color) and chlorophyll *b* (dark green color). During the color change, the two chlorophyll pigments are converted by enzymes into colorless molecules. The first Tetraterpenes that the orange tree synthesizes in preparation for color changes are phytoene and phytofluene. Both of these are colorless and are the precursor molecules to all colorful Carotenes and Carotenoids.

The unripe orange fruit makes a color change (**color break**) triggered by cooler daytime and nighttime temperatures. Phytoene and phytofluene are converted into low concentrations of *beta*-carotene (yellow-orange color), *alpha*-carotene (yellow color), lutein (yellow color), and *trans*-violaxanthin (yellow color). The green chlorophyll pigments begin to degrade (green color vanishes) as the yellow and orange Tetraterpenes are produced. The orange fruit makes the color break from green to yellow-green.

During the next three months as the fruit ripens from within, the orange fruit takes on a distinct yellow color. There are stable concentrations of *beta*-carotene (yellow-orange color), *alpha*-carotene (yellow color), lutein (yellow color), and *trans*-violaxanthin (yellow color) to keep the peel looking yellow.

Just four months before the orange fruits are harvested, there is a significant change in the Tetraterpene and Oxygenated Tetraterpene molecules present in the peel. There is a rapid drop in *beta*-carotene (yellow-orange color), lutein (yellow color), and *alpha*-carotene (yellow color). At the same time, there is a rapid rise in *trans*-violaxanthin (yellow color) and 9-*cis*-violaxanthin (yellow-orange color). These changes cause the fruit to take on a full-yellow color with a slightly orange tinge.

With only three months before harvest, the orange fruits continue their color transition. There is another rise in the colorless phytoene precursor. There is also a continual rise in zeaxanthin (yellow-orange color), 9-*cis*-violaxanthin (yellow-orange color), and the first appearance of *beta*-cryptoxanthin (orange color). There is also a moderate rise in *trans*-violaxanthin (yellow color). Then there is a significant continual drop in *alpha*-carotene (yellow color), *beta*-carotene (yellow-orange color), and lutein (yellow color). These pigment changes result in a deep yellow and slightly orange-colored fruit.

During the last two months as the fruit sweetens, the orange peel takes on its final color; a solid yellow with an orange background. During the fruit sweetening months, there is a continual rise in phytoene (colorless), *trans*-violaxanthin (yellow color), 9-*cis*-violaxanthin (yellow-orange color), and *beta*-cryptoxanthin (orange color). The most abundant carotenoid in mature orange fruit is 9-*cis*-violaxanthin (yellow-orange color). The levels of lutein (yellow color) and zeaxanthin (yellow-orange) remain stable. The Tetraterpenes *alpha*-carotene (yellow color) and *beta*-carotene (yellow-orange color) drop to near-zero levels.

In the final month, some orange varieties produce *zeta*-carotene (cream color) or *beta*-citraurin (red) pigments just before the orange fruits are ready to harvest. The total quantity of Tetraterpene and Oxygenated Tetraterpene molecules nearly doubles each month during the final three months of ripening.

- **Immature fruit:** chlorophyll *a* (light green color), chlorophyll *b* (dark green color), phytoene (colorless), and phytofluene (colorless).
- **Color break:** *beta*-carotene (yellow-orange color), *alpha*-carotene (yellow color), lutein (yellow color), and *trans*-violaxanthin (yellow color).
- **Ripening fruit:** *trans*-violaxanthin (yellow color) and 9-*cis*-violaxanthin (yellow-orange color)

- **Mature fruit:** zeaxanthin (yellow-orange color), 9-*cis*-violaxanthin (yellow-orange color), and *beta*-cryptoxanthin (orange color)

These colorful Tetraterpene and Oxygenated Tetraterpene molecules are retained in cold-pressed orange oils. These large molecules do not evaporate from the skin or other surfaces.

Color Molecules in Grapefruit Oil

There are three color varieties of grapefruits (*Citrus paradisi*) that are produced for juice and essential oils. They are commonly known as white grapefruit, pink grapefruit, and red grapefruit. The color of the peel is an indication of unique combinations of Carotenes and Carotenoids.

In mature white grapefruit, the colorless phytoene and phytofluene molecules make up about 75% of the peel Carotenes and Carotenoids. In pink grapefruit, the major color molecules are lycopene (red color) and *beta*-carotene (orange color). In red grapefruit, the final red color of the fruit comes from lycopene (red color).

It is common to mix two or three colored varieties of grapefruits in cold-pressed grapefruit essential oil. Sometimes grapefruit oil appears yellow in color while other times it appears pink or reddish. It is economical to have this color variation in cold-pressed grapefruit oil.

Color Molecules in Lemon Oil

Eureka lemons are the most common variety of lemons (*Citrus limon*). In the first 4-5 months of fruit development, they are green-colored from the chlorophyll molecules. The color breaks about 7 months prior to harvest when the lemon transitions from green, to green-yellow, to yellow-pale green, and to yellow in color. In the final month before harvest, lemon fruits take on a deeper yellow color. These are the 40-Carbon color molecules that end up in cold-pressed lemon essential oil.

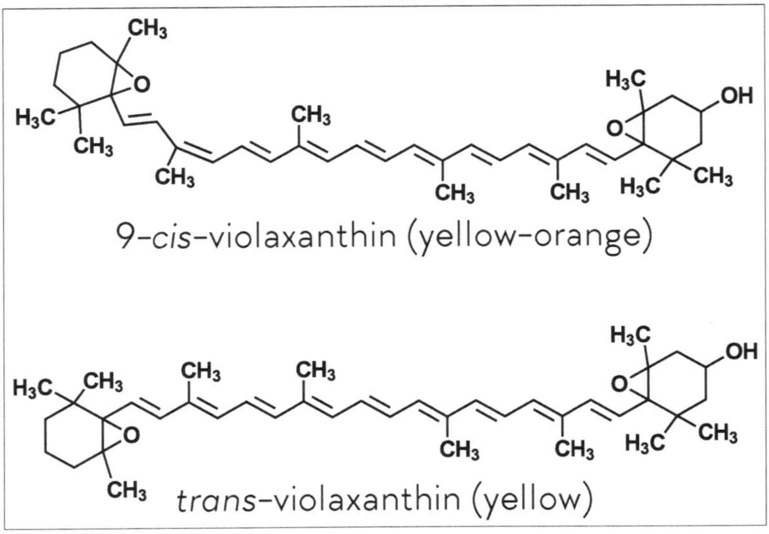

9-*cis*-violaxanthin (yellow-orange)

trans-violaxanthin (yellow)

Figure 40. Biochemical structures of Oxygenated Tetraterpene Oxide pigment molecules.

- **Immature fruit:** chlorophyll *a* (light green color), chlorophyll *b* (dark green color)
- **Color break:** *beta*-carotene (yellow-orange color), *alpha*-carotene (yellow color), and lutein (yellow color)
- **Ripening fruit:** *zeta*-carotene (cream color), *beta*-cryptoxanthin (orange color) and phytoene (colorless)
- **Mature fruit:** *delta*-carotene (red-orange)

Color Molecules in Lime Oils

The major pigments that provide the green color of cold-pressed lime essential oils (*Citrus aurantifolia* and *Citrus latifolia*) are chlorophyll *a* (light green color) and chlorophyll *b* (dark green color). Mature lime fruits may also produce a small quantity of the Tetraterpene *beta*-carotene (orange color). By contrast, distilled lime oils are clear and colorless – an indication of the lack of chlorophyll pigments and *beta*-carotene.

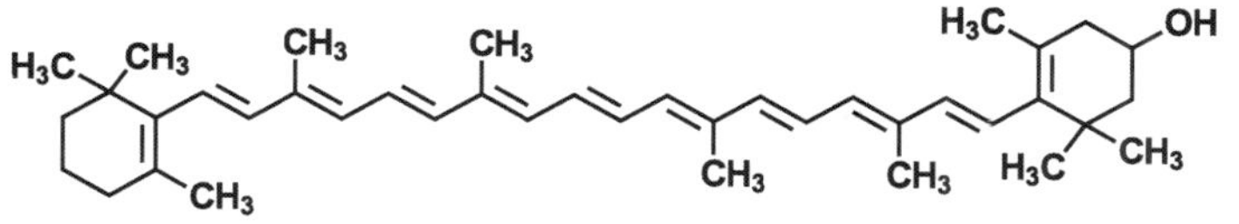

beta-cryptoxanthin (orange)

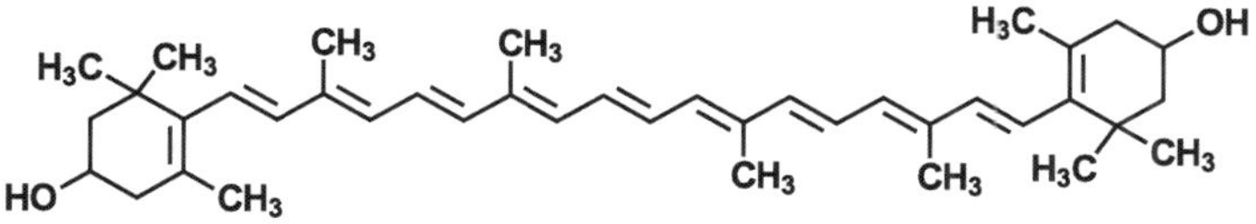

zeaxanthin (orange-yellow)

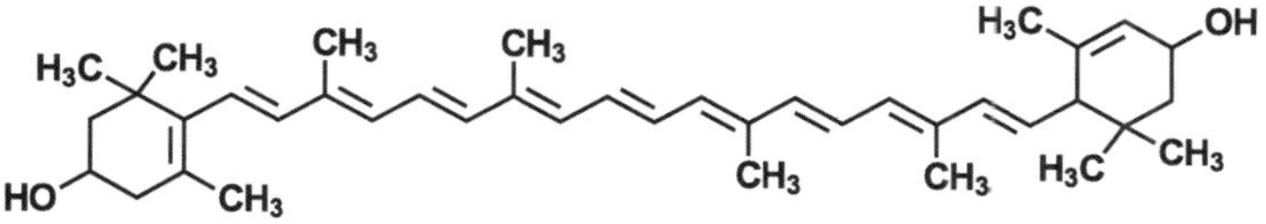

lutein (yellow)

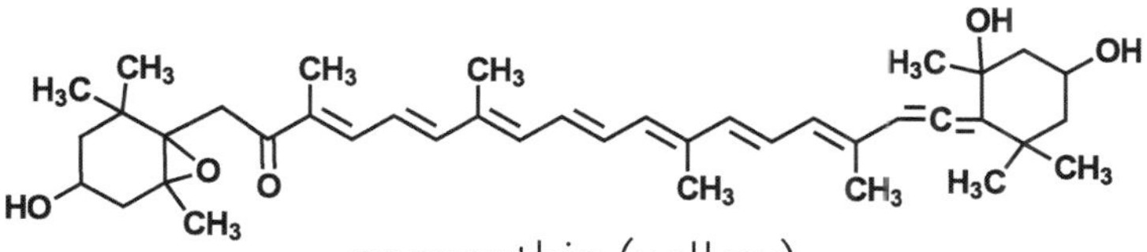

neoxanthin (yellow)

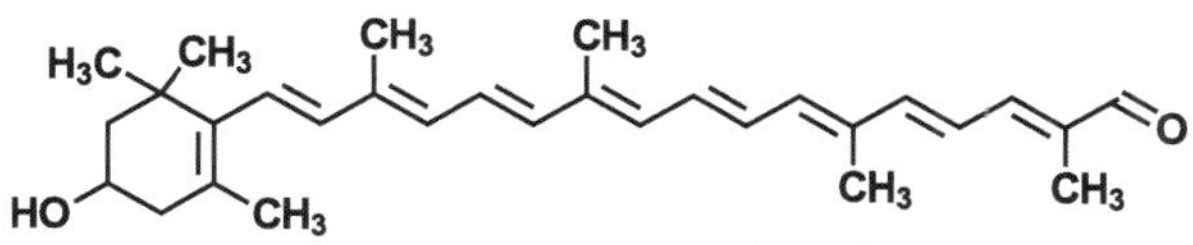

beta-citraurin (red)

Figure 41. Biochemical structures of Oxygenated Tetraterpene and Triterpene pigment molecules.

Color Molecules in Tangerine Oil

Tangerines (sometimes referred to as *Citrus tangerina*) are a subclass of Mandarin oranges (*Citrus reticulata*). There are hundreds of varieties of Mandarin citrus fruit including the most popular: mandarin, tangerine, clementine, Dancy, *satsuma (unshiu)*, Cleopatra, tangor, tangelo, and *ponkan*. Tangerines get their name from the Moroccan port of Tangiers. Mandarin fruits are typically flat on two ends and have a loose, easy-to-separate peel that is a favorite for children. The color of mature tangerines is typically orange-red, while other mandarin varieties are commonly solid orange in color.

- **Immature fruit:** chlorophyll *a* (light green color) and chlorophyll *b* (dark green color).
- **Color break:** *alpha*-carotene (yellow color), *beta*-carotene (yellow-orange color), and lutein (yellow color).
- **Ripening fruit:** *trans*-violaxanthin (yellow color), 9-*cis*-violaxanthin (yellow-orange color), *beta*-cryptoxanthin (orange color), and zeaxanthin (orange-yellow color)
- **Mature fruit:** *beta*-cryptoxanthin (orange color), *zeta*-carotene (cream color) and *beta*-citraurin (red color)

These cold-pressed citrus oils are economical because they are produced as a side-product of the citrus juicing process. Roughly 80% of all citrus oils are used in the soft-drink and juice industries. Tangerine, orange, lemon, lime, and mandarin are used as natural flavors in cola and lemon-lime soft drinks.

Color Molecules in Mandarin Oil

Mandarins (*Citrus reticulata*) encompass a wide variety of small, easy-to-peel citrus fruits. Mandarin oranges are typically orange to deep-orange in color. The developing mandarin fruit starts out green-colored like other citrus fruits and then goes through a color change 5-6 months prior to harvest.

- **Immature fruit:** chlorophyll *a* (light green color) and chlorophyll *b* (dark green color).
- **Color break:** *alpha*-carotene (yellow color) and *beta*-carotene (yellow-orange color), and lutein (yellow color).
- **Ripening fruit:** 9-*cis*-violaxanthin (yellow-orange color)
- **Mature fruit:** *beta*-citraurin (red color)

TETRATERPENES AND OXYGENATED TETRATERPENES – HEALTH AND DIFFUSION

Tetraterpene and Oxygenated Tetraterpene molecules can be beneficial to the body. When ingested, these molecules act as **antioxidants** to help protect the body from harmful chemicals, promote normal cardiovascular fitness, and support normal cellular health. They can also slow down the **free radical aging** process. They also help promote good cardiovascular health and maintain normal healthy cells.

When diffusing cold-pressed citrus oils, you may experience residual yellow, orange, red, or green stains. These stains are caused by the Tetraterpene and Oxygenated Tetraterpene molecules that do no evaporate from cold-pressed citrus oils. When these color stains accumulate in diffuser devices, they can create a sticky gum that can damage the diffuser, especially ultrasonic diffusers.

EXPLORING SUMMARY

- The 40-Carbon Tetraterpene molecules are known for their color, not for their aroma.
- Tetraterpenes are also known as Carotenes.
- Oxygenated Tetraterpenes are also referred to as Carotenoids.
- Tetraterpenes are never found in steam distilled and hydro-distilled essential oils.
- Triterpene and Tetraterpene molecules can be found in cold-pressed citrus essential oils.

GLOSSARY

Tetraterpene: A 40-Carbon essential oil molecule formed by connecting 4 terpenes units. "Tetra-" means "four" and "-terpene" means "10-Carbon molecule".

Carotenes (CARE-ahh-teens): Large Tetraterpene hydrocarbon molecules containing 40 Carbon atoms and a number of Hydrogen atoms.

Oxygenated Tetraterpenes: A 40-Carbon essential oil molecule that contains at least one Oxygen atom.

Carotenoids (car-AHH-ten-oids): Oxygenated Tetraterpene molecules that "look like" Carotene molecules. They contain 40 Carbon atoms, a number of Hydrogen atoms, and 1-6 Oxygen atoms.

Pigment: Tetraterpene (Carotene) and Oxygenated Tetraterpene (Carotenoid) molecules that are known for their natural green, yellow, orange, and redcolors in citrus peels.

Color Break: A distinct change in the peel color of maturing citrus fruits.

Antioxidants: Molecules that slow down or quench free-radical molecules.

Free Radical Aging: A process where one free radical (usually Oxygen gas radical) steals an electron from a molecule in the body. This results in the aging of the body. Signs of aging include wrinkled skin, tough skin, damaged skin, and poorly functioning organs to name a few.

DR. WOOLLEY'S CHALLENGE

- Copy two chemical structures of Tetraterpene molecules and two chemical structures of Oxygenated Tetraterpene molecules. Write down their chemical names.
- Write a paragraph discussing why large Tetraterpene molecules are not typically found in steam distilled and hydro-distilled essential oils.
- Explain to a child or adult why Tetraterpene molecules are known for their colors and not for their aromas.
- Explain to a child or adult the function of Tetraterpene and Oxygenated Tetraterpene molecules in creating color changes in citrus fruit.

12

Collecting Distilled Essential Oils

Plants produce a wide range of essential oil molecules within their specialized trichomes, secretory sacs, and resin canals. Industrial collection methods attempt to collect all the essential oil molecules, but some methods fail in their attempts. The most common industrial collection methods are Steam Distillation, Hydro-distillation, and Cold-Pressing.

Steam Distillation and Hydro-distillation collect about 50-80% of the plant-produced molecules, mainly Monoterpenes, Oxygenated Monoterpenes, Sesquiterpenes, and Oxygenated Sesquiterpenes. These two steam-temperature collection techniques leave the heavier molecules in the plant material: Diterpenes, Triterpenes and Tetraterpenes. Cold-Pressing is used mainly to express citrus fruit oils. However, because it is a mechanical collection technique, it provides recovery of all essential oil molecules in the citrus peel, from Monoterpenes to Tetraterpenes.

This chapter will help you understand the two distillation methods used to collect essential oil molecules from plants, roots, trees, branches, leaves, and oleogum-resins.

STEAM DISTILLATION

Steam Distillation is the most common process for collecting essential oil from harvested plants. Steam Distillation is performed for harvested plant stems, leaves, dried roots, fresh flowers, and chipped wood. Steam Distillation is commonly used because the equipment costs are affordable. If natural gas is not available, then wood, dried grass, diesel, or coal is used to heat up water in the steam boiler.

The set-up process for Steam Distillation is relatively simple: Harvest the plant material and let it dry for 1-3 days. Make sure the **steam boiler** is running hot. Place the plant material in the **distillation vat**. Compact the plant material so the steam will evenly heat the entire mass. Turn the valve to start the steam flowing through the plant material. Secure the lid on top and connect the **gooseneck** and **vapor line** between the lid and **cooling condenser**. Turn on the cooling water to chill the cooling condenser. The most common cooling condensers are **shell-in-tube condensers** and **coiled tube condensers**.

Depending on the steam flow rate and the mass of plant material, the first drops of condensed **hydrosol** and condensed essential oil will drip from the **condensate line** into the **separator** about 30 minutes after the lid is secured. It takes another 2-3 hours to complete most Steam Distillations.

The separation process occurs between the condensed essential oil and the condensed hydrosol in the separator. Most essential oils float on water. Since hydrosol is simply the condensed steam water mixed with some water-soluble essential oil molecules, then the essential oil floating layer occurs quickly and is very distinct.

The Steam Distillation shut-down process starts by discontinuing the steam flow through the plant material. The gooseneck vapor line is disconnected from the lid and condenser when it is safe. The lid is carefully opened to release the trapped steam. The distilled plant material is removed from the vat and composted on the farm. Now the Steam Distillation system is ready for another batch. If a different species of plant is being distilled, it is best to fully clean out the empty system with steam.

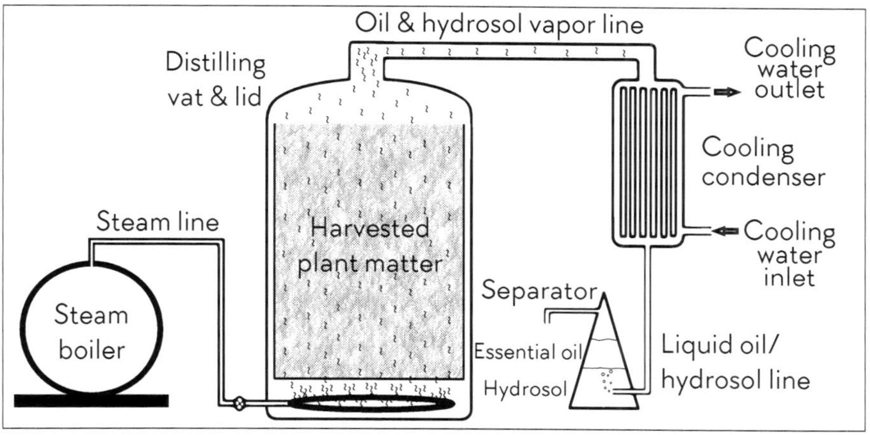

Figure 42. Schematic drawing of the Steam Distillation equipment and process.

There are limitations to the Steam Distillation technique. The major limitation is the maximum temperature of the steam at 212°F (100°C). Steam Distillation can only release the smaller molecules from the full range of molecules that the plant produces. The following list displays the approximate collection efficiency of Steam Distillation.

- Monoterpenes and Oxygenated Monoterpenes = 90-100%
- Sesquiterpenes and Oxygenated Sesquiterpenes = 30-70%
- Diterpenes = 1-20%
- Triterpenes = less than 1%
- Tetraterpenes = 0%

When distilled residue plant material (compost) is taken out of the distillation vat it still contains trace quantities of Sesquiterpenes and abundant quantities of Diterpene, Triterpene, and Tetraterpene molecules. The only way to collect higher percentages of these heavy essential oil molecules is to continue the Steam Distillation process for another 2-100 hours. Unfortunately, the extra Steam Distillation time marginally assists in collecting additional heavy molecules. The major reason that extra distillation time is not usually performed has to do with the high cost of operation and the low essential oil yield.

Distillation managers watch the volume of essential oil distilled every 15 minutes. When they plot the results, they usually find that most of the essential oil volume is collected in the first 90 minutes. During the final 90 minutes of a 3-hour Steam Distillation, the essential oil yield volume dramatically drops. Therefore, 90% of the essential oil volume is typically collected in the first 90 minutes while only 10% of the volume is collected in the final 90 minutes. Continuing the distillation for a third 90 minutes may only tally an additional 1% to the collected essential oil volume.

Continuing the Steam Distillation process will yield lower and lower volumes every hour. In contrast, the quality of the essential oil increases with every hour of Steam Distillation as higher percentages of Sesquiterpene, Oxygenated Sesquiterpene, and Diterpene molecules enter the collected essential oil. However, the operational costs to obtain increased volumes are usually too high for distillation managers to justify the cost. Some common examples of steam distilled essential oils are: Wood oils, Perennial oils, and Spice oils

HYDRO-DISTILLATION

With Hydro-distillation, steam is produced by boiling water in the distillation vat. The Hydro-distillation process is commonly used for collecting essential oils from oleogum-resins of frankincense, elemi, and myrrh.

Hydro-distillation of oleogum-resins is relatively simple. Pour water in the distillation vat. Heat the water and dispense in a measured quantity of oleogum-resin. Secure the lid, connect the vapor line to the condenser, and start the distillation by heating the base of the vat. Natural gas powered flame heaters are very common. In remote locations wood, coal, or dried grass is used for fuel. Heat up the base of the Hydro-distillation vat in order to boil the water at 212°F (100°C) and generate steam.

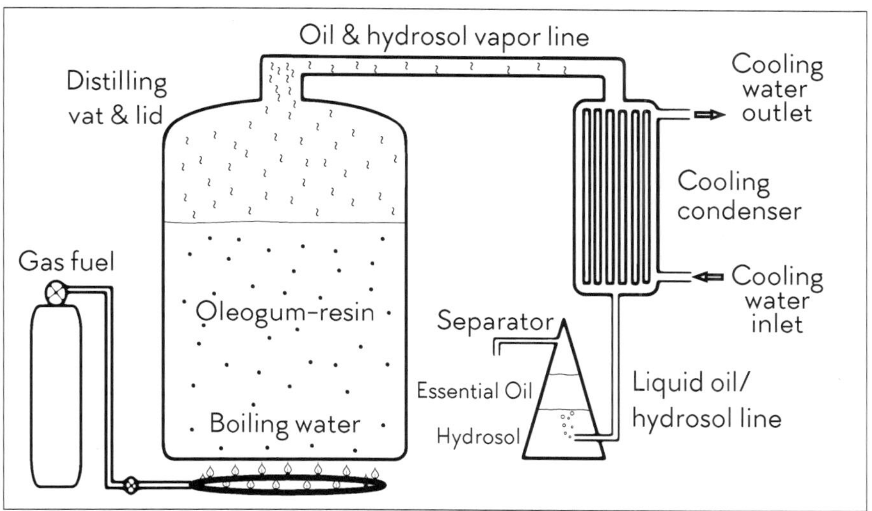

Figure 43. Schematic drawing of the Hydro-distillation equipment and process.

As the process begins to produce steam, the chunks of oleogum-resin fall apart and melt. The water-soluble gum portion circulates in the currents of boiling water. The water-insoluble essential oil molecules and very large resin molecules form a bubbling froth that floats on top. During the first 60 minutes, the essential oil molecules escape from the bubbling froth, then condense and collect in the separator. As the bubbling froth loses significant quantities of essential oil, the density of the resin increases beyond the density of water. Small balls of resin begin to fall out of the bubbling froth. Eventually the resin balls lose more essential oil, combine with other resin balls, and permanently drop to the bottom of the vat.

At the end of the Hydro-distillation of oleogum-resins, the murky water in the kettle contains the dissolved gum portion, while the Separator contains the condensed liquid essential oil and liquid hydrosol. The solid, molten resin portion fills the lower part of the Hydro-distillation vat.

The Hydro-distillation technique is limited to collect the range of smaller molecules stored in plant trichomes, secretory sacs, and resin canals. The collected molecules from Hydro-distillation are nearly the same as for Steam Distillation because the maximum steam temperature is the same at 212°F (100°C). In hydro-distilled oleogum-resin essential oils, it is typical to find high levels of Monoterpenes and Oxygenated Monoterpenes, slightly lower levels of Sesquiterpenes and Oxygenated Sesquiterpenes, and low levels of Diterpenes and Oxygenated Diterpenes. These are the typical collection efficiencies for a 3-hour Hydro-distillation of frankincense oleogum-resin:

- Monoterpenes and Oxygenated Monoterpenes = 90-100%
- Sesquiterpenes and Oxygenated Sesquiterpenes = 30-70%
- Diterpenes = 1-20%
- Triterpenes = less than 1%
- Tetraterpenes = 0%

This information is critical because most oleogum-resins contain high percentages (20-30%) of heavy Diterpene, Oxygenated Diterpene, Triterpene, and Oxygenated Triterpene molecules. The only way to collect more of the Sesquiterpene, Diterpene and Triterpene molecules is to run the Hydro-distillation unit for a total of 8, 12, or 16 hours, sometimes even more. Although the essential oil volume yields are considerably low for each subsequent hour of Hydro-distillation, the aroma and bioactivity of the frankincense essential oil is richer in Sesquiterpene, Oxygenated Sesquiterpene, and Diterpene molecules!

The strong "woody" and "earthy" aromas from the distilled residue of frankincense and myrrh resins remaining in the Hydro-distillation vat is an indication of the abundance of residual heavy molecules. The **maximum temperature of steam** is 212°F (100°C) at low pressures. Therefore, Steam Distillation and Hydro-distillation are **selective collections** of the smaller molecules in plant matter and oleogum-resins. These two 212°F (100°C) steam-based distillations techniques are poor at collecting the heavy molecules (Triterpenes and Tetraterpenes) that plants produce.

SUPERCRITICAL FLUID EXTRACTION

A less-common method for extracting Triterpenes from oleogum-resins is called Supercritical Fluid Extraction (SFE). Supercritical Fluid Extraction is not a distillation method. SFE utilizes high pressure Carbon Dioxide gas to extract larger essential oil molecules. With Supercritical Fluid Extraction, the larger molecules (Sesquiterpenes, Diterpenes, and Triterpenes) are selectively collected, while the smaller molecules (Monoterpenes) are lost when the Carbon Dioxide gas in the pressurized SFE chamber is released.

EXPLORING SUMMARY

- Steam Distillation is a process for collecting essential oil molecules from plant material.
- The essential oil molecules are energized by the introduction of water steam at 212°F (100°C) to leave plant material as vapor molecules, then transformed from vapor molecules into liquid molecules by a cooling condenser, and collected in a separator.

- Hydro-distillation is a process where plant material (usually oleogum-resin) is boiled in water in order to energize the essential oil molecules at the steam temperature of 212°F (100°C).
- Essential oils that are steam distilled or hydro-distilled are chiefly limited to Monoterpene, Oxygenated Monoterpene, Sesquiterpene, and Oxygenated Sesquiterpene, and Diterpene molecules due to the maximum temperature of steam at 212°F (100°C).

GLOSSARY

Steam Distillation: An industrial process for releasing essential oil molecules (Monoterpenes to Diterpenes) from plant matter using steam at 212°F (100°C) from a steam generator.

Hydro-distillation: An industrial process for releasing essential oil molecules (Monoterpenes to Diterpenes) from oleogum-resins boiled in water at 212°F (100°C) within a distillation vat.

Steam Boiler: A hot water heater that brings water to the boiling point of 212°F (100°C). The boiler uses fossil fuels (diesel, gasoline, or coal) or renewable fuels (dried grass, dried distilled material, or wood chips) as a source of energy.

Distillation Vat: A large stainless steel container used to temporarily store harvested plant material to be distilled.

Gooseneck: A typically smooth-angled stainless steel tube that connects to the lid of the distillation vat and the hot vapor line that feeds the cooling condenser.

Cooling Condenser: The portion of the distillation device that has an outer jacket that is cooled with cold water. The water-cooled condenser transforms hot steam vapors and hot essential oil vapors into liquid hydrosol and liquid essential oil, respectively.

Shell-in-Tube Condenser: A series of parallel tubes welded in a bundle to allow hot distillation vapors to flow through the tubes and cold water to circulate around the individual tubes.

Coiled Tube Condenser: A single, long tube that is coiled like a spring to allow hot distillation vapors to flow through the tube and cold water to circulate around the coiled tube.

Hydrosol: The condensed liquid water in the separator. Hydrosol starts out as steam vapor and is condensed into liquid water. Hydrosol contains essential oil molecules (usually Oxygenated Monoterpenes) that are attracted to water molecules.

Separator: A container that collects condensed liquid hydrosol and liquid essential oil. Essential oil is usually less dense than water allowing the oil to float on water.

Maximum Temperature of Steam: Water boils at 212°F (100°C). Liquid water is converted into vapor water (steam) at 212°F (100°C).

Selective Collection: A process limited to collecting a specific range of essential oil molecules.

DR. WOOLLEY'S CHALLENGE

- Draw or copy the diagram of the mechanics of the Steam Distillation process. Label the major pieces. Draw and label the steam generator, distiller vat, steam line, vapor line, condenser, condensed liquid line, steam vapor, plant matter, essential oil vapor, hydrosol vapor, separator, essential oil liquid, and hydrosol liquid.
- Draw or copy the diagram of the mechanics of the Hydro-distillation process. Label the major pieces. Draw and label the distiller vat, water in vat, vapor line, condenser, condensed liquid line, steam vapor, oleogum-resin, essential oil vapor, hydrosol vapor, separator, essential oil liquid, and hydrosol liquid.

13

Collecting Cold-Pressed Essential Oils

COLD-PRESS EXPRESSION

Historically, citrus juice was prepared by manually slicing the fruit and pressing each half onto inverted wooden cones to express the juice. The peel was collected in a separate bin. In Italy, where citrus fruits are plentiful, the empty half-fruit peels were soaked in water, then enveloped in a large sponge where the peel was individually pressed against a polished wooden post to express the essential oil into the sponge. The sponge was routinely rinsed in water to release the essential oil. This is an example of traditional **Cold-Press** technology.

Prior to World War II, citrus juice producers began taking a closer look at automating the juicing process. At the time, juicing and cold-pressing were still considered separate processes. The demand for citrus oils in the production of store-bought juices, soda pop drinks, and foods helped create an expanding market for cold-pressed citrus essential oils.

Today, there are four major industrial processes that are considered **expression** techniques for collecting citrus essential oils. All four industrial Cold-Press methods collect citrus juice and citrus essential oil. There are instructional videos on the internet depicting each of these industrial Cold-Press techniques for citrus oils.

It will be valuable for you to understand the range of essential oil molecules that are collected from cold-pressed citrus peels. Unlike Steam Distillation and Hydro-distillation that limit the collection to mostly Monoterpenes, Oxygenated Monoterpenes, Sesquiterpenes, and Oxygenated Sesquiterpenes, these four Cold-Press techniques produce the full range of molecules from Monoterpenes to Tetraterpenes that the citrus fruit produces.

Sfumatrice Method (Juice Fruit then Fold Peel)

The Sfumatrice Method originated in Italy. Sfumatrice (Italian for "slow folding", pronounced: SA-fu-ma-TREE-chay) is the process of expressing the citrus oil from previously juiced peels. The Sfumatrice Method is commonly used throughout the Mediterranean region including Italy, Spain, Morocco, Egypt, Israel, Turkey, and Greece.

The Sfumatrice Method is part of a total juicing process referred to as Birillatrice (pronounced BEE-reel-a-TREE-chay) where citrus fruits are sliced in half and individually juiced with a rotating cone-shaped reamer. The Sfumatrice oil expression process follows the Birillatrice juicing process. The **Birillatrice-Sfumatrice Process** is very similar to the traditional hand juicing method and manual citrus peel oil expression method.

In the Sfumatrice process, the previously juiced peels are fed into a rotating drum where the peels are forced to bend and gently squeeze, without ripping or tearing, to release the citrus essential oil from the secretory sacs. You can perform the Sfumatrice process at home by gently bending or pinching a citrus peel in your hand to express the essential oil as fine sprays or mists.

Pelatrice Method (Rasp Peel then Juice Fruit)

The Pelatrice Method also originated in Italy just prior to World War II. The Pelatrice Method is commonly used in Europe, Africa, and the Middle East.

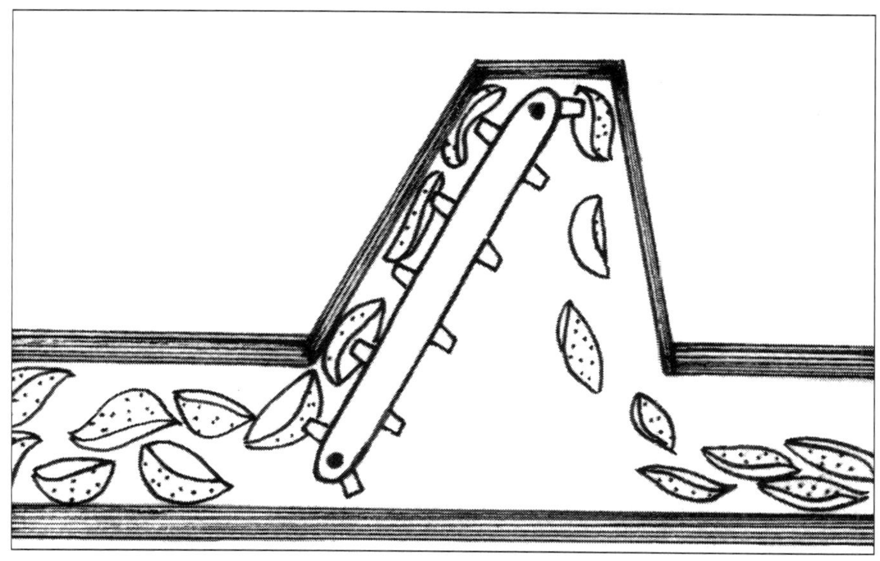

Figure 44. Schematic drawing of the Sfumatrice Cold-Press equipment and process.

Pelatrice (Italian for "peeler", pronounced: pel-a-TREE-chay) is the process where juicing occurs AFTER the oil expression process. The Pelatrice process takes the whole fruit through a large Archimedes screw where the screw surface is covered with thousands of rasping protrusions that rip the essential oil sacs off the peel surface. The rasped fruit is also sprayed with water to collect the released essential oil. In some Pelatrice machinery, the rasped whole fruit moves over more rasp-like rollers where additional essential oil is released and washed with water. The whole fruits then follow the traditional method of being sliced in half and the individual fruit-halves are mechanically juiced with rotating cone-shaped reamers.

Citrus oils collected from the Sfumatrice and Pelatrice Methods are "polished" or "finished" by taking out the small peel particles (usually by using centrifuges) and the natural waxes (by chilling the oil until the waxes become solid). This process is referred to as **citrus oil finishing** or **citrus oil polishing**. The finished citrus oils are clear and transparent. The color of these cold-pressed oils are the result of Tetraterpene and Oxygenated Tetraterpene pigment molecules collected during the Cold-Press processing.

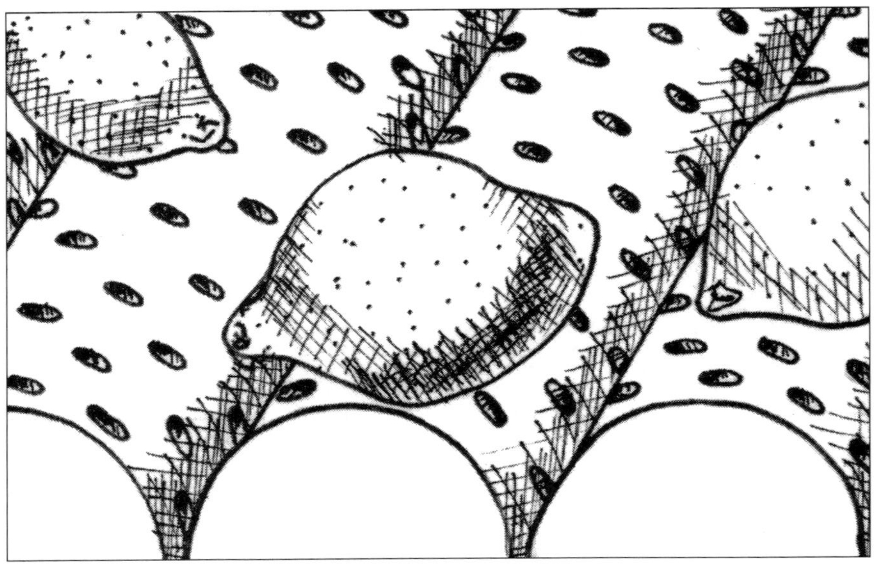

Figure 45. Schematic drawing of the Pelatrice Cold-Press equipment and process.

The citrus oils obtained by the Sfumatrice and Pelatrice Methods contain molecules ranging from Monoterpenes to Tetraterpenes. These citrus oils also contain important aldehyde molecules, such as octanal, nonanal, decanal, undecanal, and dodecanal; that are critical to the flavor and aroma.

Brown Method (Puncture Peel then Juice Fruit)

The Brown Method is the most common Cold-Press citrus oil method in North America, Central America, South America, Asia, and Australia. With the Brown Method, truckloads of citrus fruit can be processed in one day to prepare huge tanks of citrus juice and citrus essential oil. The Brown Method is a continuous process with many stainless steel rollers that transport the citrus fruit along completely automated processing lines.

The steps of the Brown Method are: citrus harvest, citrus fruit transportation to juicing facility, unloading citrus fruit, eliminating branches and leaves, washing citrus fruit, releasing citrus oil by puncturing the peel with spiked rollers, sorting citrus fruit by size, cutting fruit in half, individually juicing fruit-halves, collecting citrus juice, and collecting solid waste.

In 1976, a company called Brown International harmonized the juicing and cold-pressing techniques into one industrial process. The citrus oil is collected from the peel of the whole fruit using stainless steel rollers with needle-like, prickly surfaces. These sharp points puncture the secretory oil sacs in the citrus fruit peel to release the citrus essential oil. Brown International calls this method Brown Oil Extraction (BOE).

The essential oil is released when the citrus fruit is continuously rolled over thousands of sharp points on stainless steel rollers while being partially submerged in a bath of water. Similar technologies use fast rotating, rasping rollers that produce small peel particles from the whole fruit while being sprayed with water. The oil-water mixture is run through a series of screens and centrifuges to take out the water, waxes, and peel fragments. These polishing steps produce a finished citrus oil that is clear and transparent. The punctured or rasped citrus fruits continue on stainless steel rollers into the juicing process where fruits are individually sliced in half and mechanically pressed for juice. Today, many large producers of orange and lemon oil use Brown International automated machinery.

Orange juice and lemon juice is usually concentrated by removing some of the water. The pulp is usually screened out and added back into brands that desire pulp. Some juice is immediately packaged as "Not From Concentrate" (NFC), while most is concentrated by evaporating off most of the water ("Frozen Concentrate Juice" – FCJ). The essential oil floating above the concentrated juice is called **"citrus essence"** (e.g., orange essence) and is usually sold to major juice brands to add a "just squeezed" flavor to the juice.

Figure 46. Schematic drawing of the Brown Cold-Press equipment and process.

The citrus oil collected from the Brown Method goes through many finishing steps to eliminate water, particles, and natural waxes. The finished oil contains the full range of molecules from Monoterpenes to Tetraterpenes. The Tetraterpene and Oxygenated Tetraterpene molecules give citrus oils their distinctive color.

FMC Method (Simultaneous Juice and Press Peel)

The FMC Method simultaneously expresses the juice and oil from the citrus fruit in one step. The FMC Method utilizes many of the same automated processes of fruit cleaning, fruit sorting, juice finishing, and essential oil finishing as the Brown Method. The FMC method is also referred to as the JBT Method since FMC was purchased by JBT. FMC equipment is used throughout the world.

In 1947, a company named Food Machinery Corporation (FMC) developed an automated citrus juice and oil extractor that revolutionized the industry. Whole citrus fruits are positioned between two stainless steel cupped jaws and are individually punctured from below with a "juice tube". As the stainless steel jaws compress, the citrus juice flows down through the "juice tube" to a juice-holding tank. At the same time, the jaw-compressed fruit releases the citrus oil from the peel and rinses the oil off the peel with jets of water. The citrus oil/water mixture is directed to a separate oil-holding tank. The citrus oil, which also contains water and peel particles, is polished through a series of centrifuges. The resulting pure essential oil is marketed as "cold-pressed". These modular FMC citrus juicers are employed by hundreds of citrus juice factories throughout the world.

Today, under the new name JBT FoodTech, the same technology is being used to extract citrus juice and citrus oil with this modern, Cold-Press technology. Many major citrus juice companies use FMC Cold-Press technology because the citrus juice and citrus oil are expressed in a single step without the two liquids coming into contact with each other.

The completely automated steps include harvesting the citrus fruit into trucks, unloading the citrus fruit, eliminating branches and leaves, washing citrus fruit, sorting citrus fruit by size, expressing citrus juice and citrus oil in one stroke, and then collecting the solid waste.

The FMC Method releases the full range of essential oil molecules produced in the citrus fruit, from Monoterpenes to Tetraterpenes. Lemon oil is yellow-colored because it contains yellow-colored Tetraterpene and Oxygenated Tetraterpene molecules.

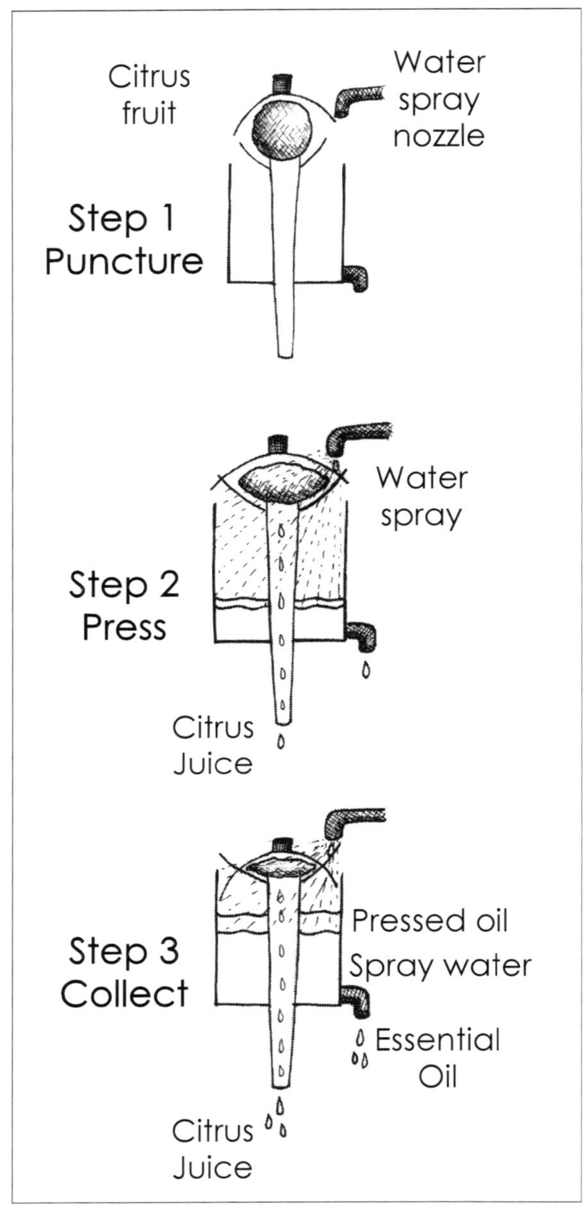

Figure 47. Schematic drawing of the puncture, press, and collect steps using the FMC Cold-Press equipment.

COLLECTION LIMITS OF DISTILLATION AND COLD-PRESS METHODS

The two distillation processes are limited in their collection capabilities by the 212°F (100°C) temperature of steam. Steam Distillation and Hydro-distillation only collect the Monoterpene, Oxygenated Monoterpene, Sesquiterpene, Oxygenated Sesquiterpene, and some of the Diterpene and Oxygenated Diterpene molecules. Unfortunately, the distilled residue plant material that is typically composted retains a majority of the Triterpene, Oxygenated Triterpene, and Tetraterpene molecules.

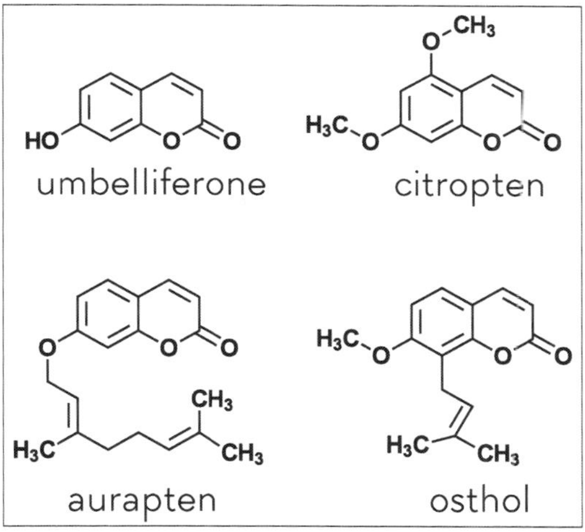

Figure 48. Biochemical structures of Coumarin molecules.

In contrast, the four Cold-Press citrus oil processes provide a full range of molecules produced in the fruit peel. Cold-pressing releases the full range of essential oils molecules, from the smallest Monoterpenes to the largest Tetraterpenes. Cold-Press methods usually collect 90-100% of the citrus oil stored in the peel. Cold-pressing citrus oils does not discriminate against the collection of the largest molecules.

COUMARINS AND FURANOCOUMARINS IN COLD-PRESSED CITRUS OILS

The Cold-Press methods collect a full range of molecules stored in citrus peels. Citrus essential oils are dominated (50-95%) by Monoterpene molecules and about 5-40% Oxygenated Monoterpene molecules. Cold-pressed citrus oils also contain about 1-2% **Coumarins** and **Furanocoumarins**. All these molecules are great for the skin except for the Coumarins and Furanocoumarins. When Coumarins and Furanocoumarins are exposed to sunlight, they cause an extreme burning, inflammation, and skin discoloring.

Citrus Coumarins is a general term of large Oxygenated molecules that are subdivided in two classes called Coumarins and Furanocoumarins. Coumarins contain a base structure possessing two fused rings. There are 9 Carbon atoms within the two fused rings and one Oxygen atom. Coumarins also contain two more Oxygen atoms, one attached with a double bond (=) as a ketone (>C=0) and the other as an alcohol (C-O-H) or ether (C-O-C).

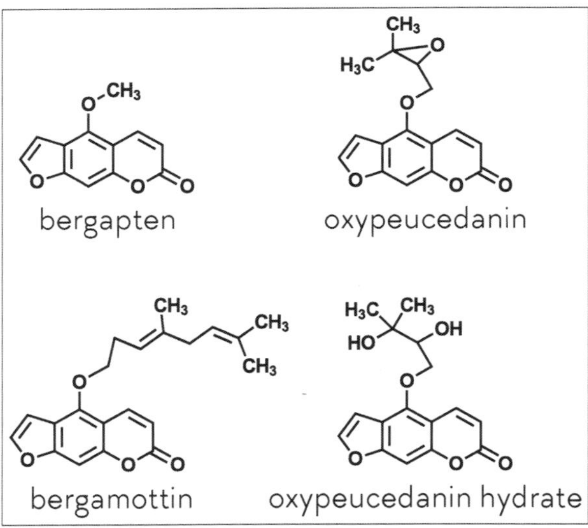

Figure 49. Biochemical structures of Furanocoumarin molecules.

The three Oxygen atoms in Coumarins make them more soluble in water and increases their retention on moist surfaces. When citrus oils are applied on your skin, the Coumarin molecules remain long after the Monoterpene and Oxygenated Monoterpene molecules evaporate.

The six most common Coumarin molecules in citrus oils are umbelliferone, aurapten, epoxyaurapten, osthol, 5-geranyloxy-7-methoxycoumarin, and limettin (citropten).

Furanocoumarins have a base structure containing three fused rings possessing 11 Carbon atoms and two Oxygen atoms. Furanocoumarins also possess one Oxygen atom as a ketone (>C=O) and 1-2 Oxygen atoms as ether groups (C-O-C). Furanocoumarins often have an Isoprene or Monoterpene group attached to one of the ether Oxygen atoms.

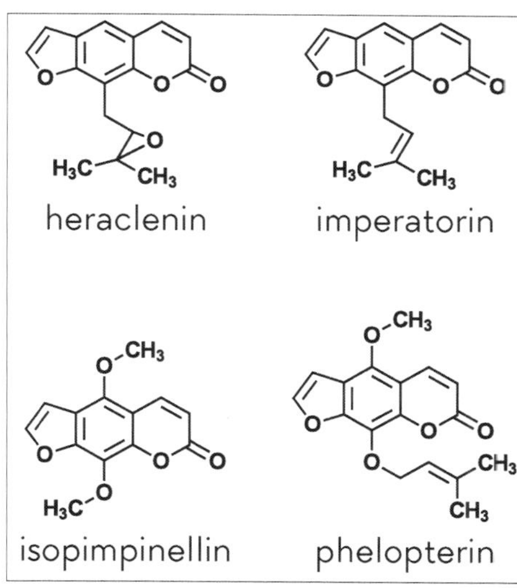

heraclenin imperatorin

isopimpinellin phelopterin

Figure 50. Biochemical structures of Furanocoumarin molecules.

Furanocoumarins are even more water-soluble and moist surface-loving than Coumarins. They love moist surfaces more because they possess 4-6 Oxygen atoms. When citrus oil molecules evaporate, only the Monoterpene, Oxygenated Monoterpenes and Sesquiterpene molecules leave the skin surface. Furanocoumarin molecules remain on the skin.

Coumarin and Furanocoumarin molecules produced in citrus fruits help fight off pathogens (bacteria and fungus). When citrus oils are ingested, these molecules may support long-life and promote normal heart health. Coumarins and Furanocoumarins also enhance the aroma and taste of cold-pressed citrus oils.

Unfortunately, Coumarins and Furanocoumarins can be harmful when applied to the skin prior to sun exposure. The most common detriment is their propensity to cause **skin photosensitivity** when exposed to sunlight. This skin burning is caused when Coumarin and Furanocoumarin molecules absorb and intensify the UV-rays of sunlight. Since Coumarin and Furanocoumarin molecules do not readily evaporate from the skin they become a safety concern.

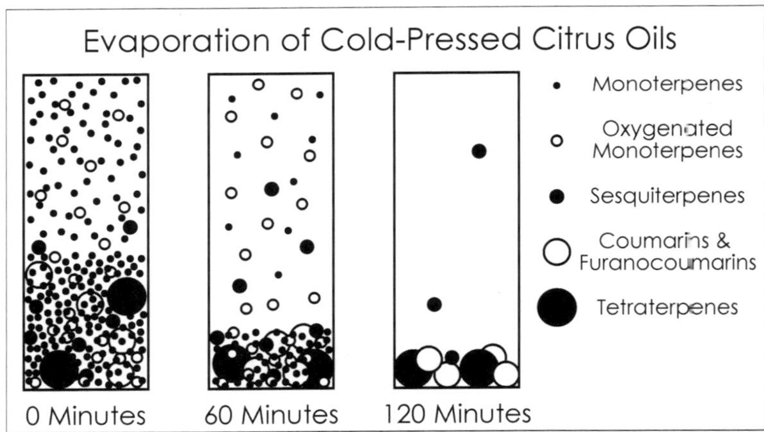

Figure 51. Time-lapse depiction for the evaporation of cold-pressed citrus essential oil molecules.

In order to help you safely apply citrus essential oils on your skin, study the chart that depicts the relative abundance of Coumarins and Furanocoumarins in cold-pressed citrus oils. The citrus oils with the lowest relative abundance are all orange-colored citrus fruits (orange, clementine, mandarin, and tangerine) and are generally safe to apply prior to sun exposure. Those with the highest relative abundance are yellow-, green-, or red-colored citrus fruits (lime, lemon, bergamot, and grapefruit) and may cause skin photosensitivity when applied prior to sun exposure. Take the greatest care when applying citrus oils with the highest concentration of Coumarins and Furanocoumarins, especially when you go outdoors in the sun.

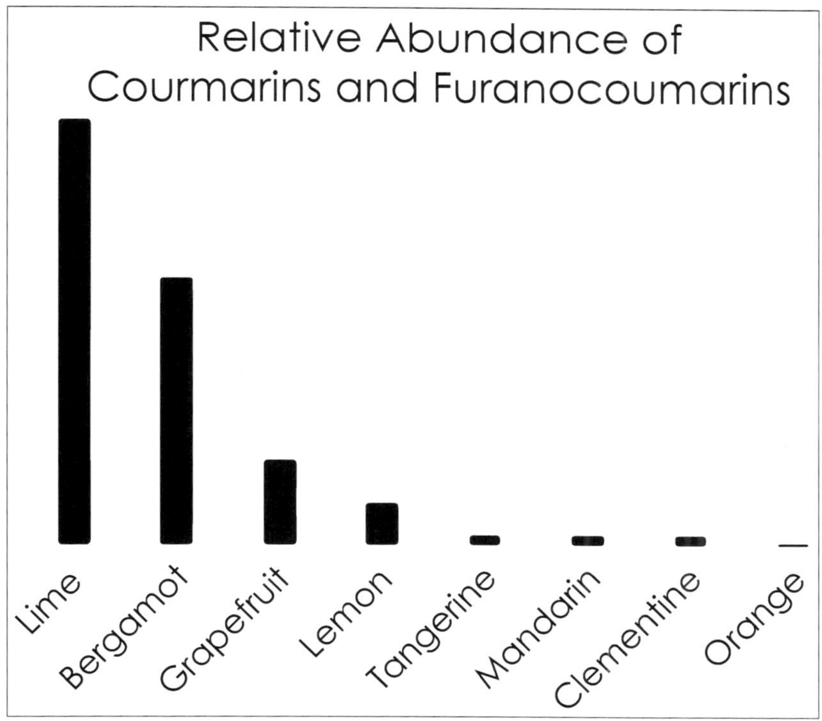

Figure 52. Diagram of the relative abundance of Coumarin and Furanocoumarin molecules in cold-pressed citrus essential oils.

Cold-pressed citrus oils with the highest relative concentration of Coumarins and Furanocoumarins can be distilled to eliminate these heavy molecules. The cold-pressed citrus oil is simply placed in a distillation vat, then heated to collect the Monoterpene, Oxygenated Monoterpene, and Sesquiterpene molecules. The heavier molecules (Coumarins, Furanocoumarins, Tetraterpenes, and Oxygenated Tetraterpenes) remain in the distillation vat as waste material.

Distilled citrus oils are commonly distinguished from the cold-pressed citrus oils with the descriptive suffix "FCF", standing for "FuranoCoumarin-Free". Bergamot oil is most commonly referred to as Bergamot FCF. These distilled citrus oils are clear and colorless because they do not contain Tetraterpene molecules. If the bergamot essential oil you are using does not specify "FCF", be careful applying it prior to sun exposure.

The safest way is the most cautious – do not apply cold-pressed citrus oils prior to enjoying the sun. Be cautious applying citrus oils on diffuser jewelry that contacts the skin. Be cautious applying essential oil blends to your skin prior to sun exposure. Read the label to see if it contains cold-pressed citrus oils. If the cold-pressed citrus oil is in high concentration, then you may want to consider the risk.

Scrubbing with soap and water will eliminate Coumarin and Furanocoumarin molecules from your skin. Alcohol wipes will also help scour Coumarin and Furanocoumarin molecules. You can rely on alcohol-based hand sanitizing liquids to dissolve and separate Coumarins and Furanocoumarins from your skin. When in doubt clean your skin prior to sun exposure to reduce your risk of skin photosensitivity caused by Coumarin and Furanocoumarin molecules.

EXPLORING SUMMARY

- There are four types of industrial Cold-Press processes for expressing essential oils from citrus peels: Sfumatrice, Pelatrice, Brown and FMC.
- The Sfumatrice Method (juice fruit then fold peel) and the Pelatrice Method (rasp peel then juice fruit) were developed

in Italy. These Cold-Press methods are commonly used to produce citrus oils in Europe, Africa, and the Middle East.

- The Brown Method (puncture peel then juice fruit) and the FMC Method (simultaneous juice and press peel) were developed in the USA. These Cold-Press methods are commonly used to express citrus oils in North America, Central America, South America, Australia, Pacific-Asia, and China.
- Cold-pressed citrus oils contain Coumarins and Furanocoumarins. Cold-pressed lime, bergamot, grapefruit and lemon contain the highest relative concentrations of these photosensitive molecules.
- Be aware to safely apply cold-pressed citrus oils to your skin prior to sun exposure. Diluting cold-pressed citrus oils (especially lime, bergamot, grapefruit, and lemon) prior to sun exposure can reduce the risk of skin photosensitivity.

GLOSSARY

Cold-Press: An industrial process for mechanically releasing essential oil molecules (Monoterpenes to Tetraterpenes) from citrus fruit peels during the citrus juicing process.

Expression: Referring to an industrial process that bends, folds, or compresses the citrus peel to release essential oil.

Smufatrice (Folding) Cold-Press Method (SA-fu-ma-TREE-chay): The Italian industrial process of bending and folding empty citrus peel halves to express essential oil from secretory sacs.

Birillatrice-Smufatrice Process (BEE-reel-a-TREE-chay): The Italian industrial process that includes citrus fruit juicing followed by Smufatrice Cold-Press essential oil expression.

Pelatrice (Rasping) Cold-Press Method (pel-a-TREE-chay): The Italian industrial process for rasping the surface of whole citrus fruit to release essential oil from secretory sacs.

Citrus Oil Finishing or Citrus Oil Polishing: Methods for cleaning up raw cold-pressed citrus oils. Centrifuges and screens are used to filter particles from the essential oil. Citrus oils are chilled, allowing the liquid essential oil to be separated from the solid natural waxes.

Brown (Puncturing) Cold-Press Method: The USA industrial process for puncturing the surface of whole citrus fruit to express essential oil from secretory sacs.

Citrus Essence: The essential oil collected from the top of expressed citrus juice. This essential oil is relatively scarce and very flavorful.

FMC (Simultaneous) Cold-Press Method: The USA industrial process for compressing whole citrus fruit for simultaneous juicing and expressing the essential oil where the juice and essential oil are instantly separated.

Coumarins (COO-mar-inz): A class of large molecules in cold-pressed citrus oils with two fused rings containing at least three Oxygen atoms.

Furanocoumarins (Fur-ANNE-OH-coo-mar-inz): A class of large molecules in cold-pressed citrus oils with three fused rings containing as least four Oxygen atoms.

Skin Photosensitivity: A skin darkening reaction and inflammation caused by Coumarin and Furanocoumarin molecules found in relatively high concentrations in some cold-pressed citrus oils.

FuranoCoumarin-Free (FCF): A designation for cold-pressed citrus oils that have been distilled to take out Coumarin and Furanocoumarin molecules.

DR. WOOLLEY'S CHALLENGE

- Watch an online video about the Brown Method (Puncturing) or FMC Method (Simultaneous) for the industrial juicing and cold-pressing of citrus oils.
- Explain to a child or adult the processing steps for the FMC (Simultaneous) Cold-Press Method including harvesting, trucking, delivery, washing, sorting, simultaneous juicing and cold-pressing, and how the juice and citrus oil flow in different channels to their holding tanks.
- Write a paragraph dealing with the health risks of applying cold-pressed citrus oils to the skin followed by sunbathing, walking in the sunlight, or sun tanning. Explain skin photosensitivity.
- Draw or copy the chemical structure of two Coumarins and two Furanocoumarins. Write the name for each molecule.
- Copy the diagram illustrating the evaporation of cold-pressed citrus oils at 0 minutes, 60 minutes, and 120 minutes.

14

Diffusing Essential Oils with Active Diffusers

One of many ways to use essential oils in your everyday life is in diffusers. You can diffuse essential oils in your home, car, office, bathroom, kitchen, and hotels. There is a variety of electrically powered essential oil diffusers on the market. I call them **Active Diffusers**. There are also a number of ways you can diffuse essential oils in your environment without using electrical diffusers (Passive Diffusers in the next chapter).

Active diffusers require some type of electrical, mechanical, or heat energy to "push" the essential oil molecules into the air. Most of these Active Diffusers require electricity. These Active Diffusers can be used in the office, car, bathroom, bedroom, kitchen, entertainment room, living room, exercise room, and den. There are four different categories of Active Diffusers; including Ultrasonic, Nebulizing, Fan, and Heat.

ULTRASONIC DIFFUSERS

Ultrasonic Diffusers are currently the most popular Active Diffusers. Ultrasonic Diffusers are similar to cold air humidifiers. They are available in a variety of styles, shapes, and colors. The water and essential oil in Ultrasonic Diffusers typically last 6-10 hours without refilling.

Operating Instructions for Ultrasonic Diffusers. Take the lid off the Ultrasonic Diffuser and add distilled, deionized, or tap water (as instructed for your diffuser) to the FILL LEVEL line indicated on the reservoir wall. Add 5-10 drops of essential oil and replace the diffuser lid. Plug in the diffuser and turn it ON. Select the available diffuser features that you want: colored lights, music, sounds, auto-OFF timer, etc.

Technical Description of Ultrasonic Diffusers. Ultrasonic Diffusers contain a stainless steel disk that vibrates millions of times per second. The most common vibrational frequency rate is 1.6 MHz (megahertz) or 1.6 million vibrations per second. The vibrating disk is positioned at the base of a water reservoir. The vibrating disk creates energetic vibrations that travel through the water and essential oil. When the disk is vibrating, the molecules of water and essential oil are energized enough to escape the liquid reservoir as airborne **micro-droplets**. These micro-droplets escape into the air as a finely dispersed mist. An electrical fan pushes the water and essential oil micro-droplets into the air above the diffuser.

Evaporation of Micro-Droplets from Ultrasonic Diffusers. The mist produced by Ultrasonic Diffusers is composed of individual water and essential oil micro-droplets. "**Soft water**" micro-droplets are typically 50-100 **micrometers** in diameter (hair diameter is about 30-70 micrometers). The micro-droplet size of "**hard water**" mist is about 150-300 micrometers in diameter. Essential oil micro-droplets are typically 25 micrometers in diameter. Water forms larger micro-droplets because water molecules have greater molecular interaction, are more compact, and form a tighter outer skin on the spherical micro-droplet surface.

The evaporation rate of essential oil molecules is quicker than water molecules. Essential oil micro-droplets undergo a rapid size

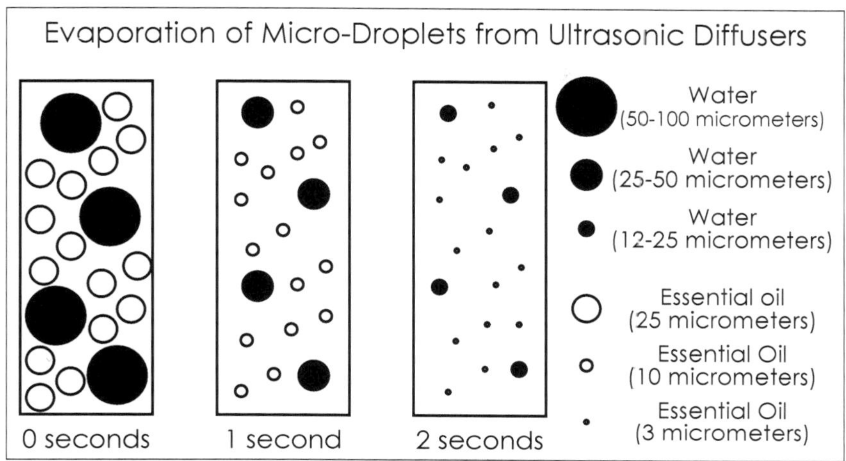

Figure 53. Time-lapse depiction of water and essential oil micro-droplets produced by Ultrasonic Diffusers.

reduction as Monoterpene molecules rapidly evaporate from its spherical surface. Essential oil molecules are loosely packed within the oil micro-droplet and readily escape from the micro-droplet surface. Essential oil micro-droplets seem to disappear from view when they shrink below 5 micrometers in diameter.

The evaporation rate of water molecules from water micro-droplets is slow because water molecules have a strong interaction and form a tight outer skin on the micro-droplet. The mist produced from Ultrasonic Diffusers is readily visible because of the abundance of water micro-droplets. The water micro-droplets slowly shrink in size as the droplets rise in the air. It takes longer for the water micro-droplets to shrink and disappear before your eyes. The water micro-droplets disappear quicker when the relative humidity is low.

Special Features of Ultrasonic Diffusers. Some Ultrasonic Diffusers have special features that add to the therapeutic effect of the essential oil mist. Some features include colored lights, soothing music, relaxing sounds, intermittent operation, and timer to shut off the diffuser. Typically, when the water dries up in the reservoir, the diffuser automatically turns itself OFF to protect the vibrating ultrasonic disk.

What People Like about Ultrasonic Diffusers. Ultrasonic Diffusers are well-liked and accepted. They come with an affordable price tag. They are also liked for their low noise level. People also like them for their constant "raindrop" sound. People also like the benefit of increased humidity in the room. Some people like the special colored lights and sound/music features. The main reason people like the Ultrasonic Diffusers is because they are simple and effective.

What People Dislike about Ultrasonic Diffusers. Ultrasonic Diffusers have their faults. The concerns of many users include: 1st = high maintenance, 2nd = short lifetime of oscillating disk, 3rd = poor water-level sensing, 4th = thick oil residue fouls the oscillating disk, 5th = scaling deposits from hard water, 6th = low-to-moderate diffuser lifespan, 7th = needing distilled water or deionized water, and 8th = electrical shorting when changing water.

Most of the Ultrasonic Diffuser users consider them "replaceable". When they quit functioning or break, they are usually tossed in the garbage. There is not much that is permanent about Ultrasonic Diffusers. Fortunately, the replacement of a nonfunctioning ultrasonic disk is simple; buy an inexpensive kit on-line, follow on-line video instructions, use a screw driver, and in less than 5 minutes you have a functioning diffuser again.

Hard Water Mineral Deposits with Ultrasonic Diffusers. If you live in an area where the tap water contains a high content of minerals, you will also experience mineral deposits on the wall of your Ultrasonic Diffuser. The most common hard water minerals are calcium and magnesium ions. They form a white-colored solid scale in bathtubs, showers, and sinks. Without regular cleaning, the mineral scale will build up and overheat the ultrasonic disk until it stops working. This hard water scale can be removed with hot vinegar. Just warm up some vinegar, pour it into the reservoir, let it sit for one hour, and use an old toothbrush to gently scrub it away.

Distilled Essential Oils with Ultrasonic Diffusers. Steam distilled and hydro-distilled essential oils completely evaporate without much residue using Ultrasonic Diffusers. The high vibration frequency easily energizes all the Monoterpene and Oxygenated Monoterpene molecules to escape into the air. The high vibrational energy also "pushes" the heavier Sesquiterpene, Oxygenated Sesquiterpene, and Diterpene molecules into the essential oil micro-droplets.

Cold-Pressed Citrus Essential Oils with Ultrasonic Diffusers. Cold-pressed citrus oils leave the most residue in Ultrasonic Diffuser reservoirs. They also cause the most damage to Ultrasonic Diffusers. Cold-pressed citrus oils are predominantly composed of small Monoterpene molecules; mainly limonene. These small molecules completely escape into the air.

Unfortunately, cold-pressed citrus oils contain large Tetraterpene, Coumarin, and Furanocoumarin molecules. Ultrasonic Diffusers do not generate enough vibrational energy to discharge these large molecules into the air. Therefore, the thick, sticky Coumarin, Furanocoumarin, and Tetraterpene molecules end up coating the reservoir and gumming up the ultrasonic disk with a sticky residue. Those who have used cold-pressed citrus oils in Ultrasonic Diffusers know that the diffuser requires periodic cleaning.

NEBULIZING DIFFUSERS

There are few Nebulizing Diffusers on the market. They are sometimes referred to as Atomizing Diffusers. Some are hand-blown from glass and others are manufactured with hardened plastics. They tend to be more expensive than other Active Diffusers. Nebulizing Diffusers are commonly used in aromatherapy and massage therapy clinics because they quickly fill the treatment room with therapeutic aroma. Unlike Ultrasonic Diffusers, there is no water involved with Nebulizing Diffusers, just pure essential oil.

Operating Instructions for Nebulizing Diffusers. To operate the most common Nebulizing Diffusers, simply screw into place any 5ml, 10ml, or 15ml bottle of essential oil, make sure the siphon tube is inserted and extends to the bottom of the essential oil bottle, and then turn the high velocity air flow adjustment to ON position. For hand-blown glass diffusers, simply fill the reservoir with your essential oil and turn on the pump. As long as there is essential oil in the bottle or reservoir, a fine mist composed of pure essential oil micro-droplets is all that you will see and smell.

Technical Description of Nebulizing Diffusers. A plastic tube, called a siphon tube, is fitted into the bottom of a bottle of essential oil. A high velocity stream of air is passed over the top of the essential oil-filled siphon tube. The high velocity air nebulizes the essential oil into micro-droplets and creates a slight vacuum within the siphon tube. The slight vacuum sucks up essential oil from the lower end of the siphon tube, like sucking on a drinking straw. The essential oil micro-droplets mix with the high velocity air to form a nearly transparent mist.

Evaporation of Micro-Droplets from Nebulizing Diffusers. The mist produced by Nebulizing Diffusers is composed solely of essential oil micro-droplets. The average micro-droplet size is 25 micrometers in diameter. The droplet size is larger (typically 30 micrometers in diameter) when the high velocity flowrate is adjusted to its highest setting. At the lowest air flow setting, the micro-droplet size is typically 10 micrometers in diameter.

The micro-droplets quickly shrink in size as the essential oil molecules evaporate into the air. When the micro-droplets shrink below 10 micrometers in diameter, they become invisible to the eye. The micro-droplet size becomes invisible to the eyes in about

1 second as the micro-droplets shrink in the rising mist. On a general note, the essential oil remaining in the bottle tends to concentrate in heavier molecules as the liquid volume diminishes.

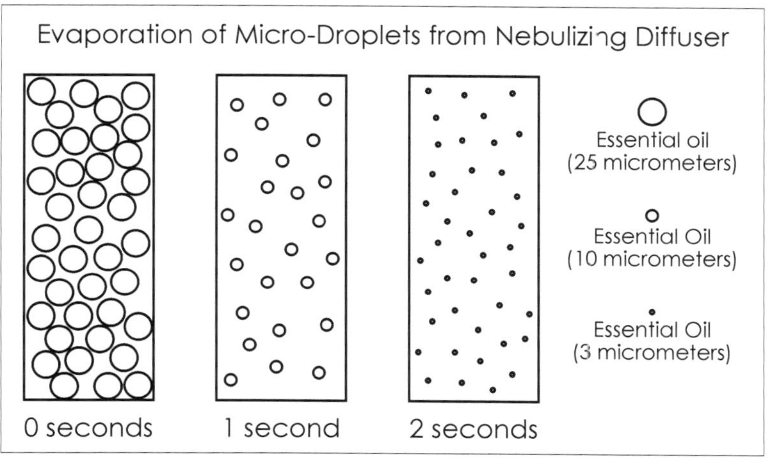

Figure 54. Time-lapse depiction of essential oil micro-droplets produced by Nebulizing Diffusers.

The mist produced by the Nebulizing Diffusers appears to be less noticeable than the mist produced by Ultrasonic Diffusers. Larger water micro-droplets produced by Ultrasonic Diffusers are more visible to the eyes and shrink at a slower rate than essential oil micro-droplets. That is why the mist from Ultrasonic Diffusers always seems more obvious and high rising.

Special Features of Nebulizing Diffusers. Some Nebulizing Diffusers have adjustments that control the velocity of the high speed air flow. The air flow knob controls the size and abundance of essential oil micro-droplets. Slow air flow equals few and small micro-droplets so a bottle of essential oil will last for days. Higher air flow creates abundant, large micro-droplets and may consume a bottle in hours.

Some Nebulizing Diffusers have time adjustments for operation. One control knob can adjust the time of intermittent operation (a time delay when air flow is OFF) and another control knob may adjust for the time the high speed air flow is ON. Another knob may adjust for automatic turnoff time. By working with these adjustments, you can control the aroma level released by the Nebulizing Diffuser and the number of hours or days of uninterrupted operation.

What People Like about Nebulizing Diffusers. People like Nebulizing Diffusers for several reasons. They can quickly fill a room with essential oil vapors without increasing the room humidity. They like the simplicity of changing essential oils; just unscrew one bottle and screw on another bottle. Very simple. People also like Nebulizing Diffusers because they do not require water.

People also like Nebulizing Diffusers because they require low maintenance. There is no oscillating disk to clean and scrub. They like that the essential oil bottle is the reservoir. They can always tell the essential oil being diffused by reading the label. The siphon tube is easy to clean with rubbing alcohol. People like Nebulizing Diffusers because they are a good investment that lasts for years.

People like the adjustment knobs to control the flow of essential oil micro-droplets. People like the ability to keep a 15ml bottle of essential oil that lasts for weeks without interruption simply by adjusting air flow to LOW, 2 minutes ON, and 20 minutes OFF. The same Nebulizing Diffuser can fill the air of a large room in minutes by adjusting flow to HIGH, 20 minutes ON, and 1 minute OFF.

What People Dislike about Nebulizing Diffusers. One common dislike about Nebulizing Diffusers is the typical higher price. People also complain that Nebulizing Diffusers are noisier than Ultrasonic Diffusers. Some complain that switching from 15ml bottles to 5ml bottles requires inserting a shorter siphon tube.

People have noticed that Nebulizing Diffusers consume essential oils too quickly. However, once they learn to properly adjust the air flow and intermittent ON/OFF controls, their negative comments cease. Also, Nebulizing Diffusers do not humidify the room, which some people find annoying.

Distilled Essential Oils with Nebulizing Diffusers. Nebulizing diffusers do an excellent job diffusing steam distilled and hydro-distilled essential oils, down to the last drop. The siphon tube sometimes gets a bit sticky from the residue of heavier molecules. Thick steam distilled and hydro-distilled oils (like valerian root and myrrh) are not easily diffused with Nebulizing Diffusers.

Cold-Pressed Citrus Essential Oils with Nebulizing Diffusers. Nebulizing Diffusers are great at diffusing cold-pressed citrus oils. However, with cold-pressed lime and lemon oils, they sometimes leave a thick residue at the bottom of the bottle. The thick residue is composed of larger molecules like Coumarins, Furanocoumarins, and Tetraterpenes. The larger molecules tend to concentrate in the last remaining liquid.

FAN DIFFUSERS

Fan Diffusers use an electrical fan to force air through a filter cartridge soaked with drops of essential oil to produce an almost invisible mist of essential oil micro-droplets. Fan Diffusers do not use water, just pure essential oil. Fan Diffusers increase the evaporation rate of essential oil molecules by forcing air around essential oil droplets absorbed on the filter cartridge. Molecules with the highest evaporation rates (Monoterpene molecules) are quickly "pushed" into the air, while molecules with lower evaporation rates (heavy Sesquiterpene and Diterpene molecules) "hesitantly" leave the filter cartridge.

Operating Instructions for Fan Diffusers. Some Fan Diffusers use AC power from the wall outlets or lower voltage USB outlets to power the fan. Others use rechargeable batteries to power the fan for portable applications. Pull out the sliding cartridge that contains the filter cartridge and add drops of essential oil. Return the filter cartridge into its operational position and turn ON the Fan Diffuser. The aroma will continue until the essential oil molecules evaporate.

Technical Description of Fan Diffusers. Fan Diffusers can greatly increase the normal evaporation rate of essential oil molecules. Tight-weave filter cartridges hold more drops of essential oils. Loose-weave filter cartridges allow more air flow. The woven fibers of the filter cartridges become coated with a thin film of essential oil molecules. The air flows through the woven micro-channels to evaporate the essential oil molecules. The air flow pushes the essential oil micro-droplets into the air above the diffuser. Filter cartridges can be quickly replaced to change essential oils. Fan Diffusers provide a quick change between diffusing lavender essential oil to diffusing peppermint essential oil; quick, easy, and low-cost.

Evaporation of Micro-Droplets from Fan Diffusers. Fan Diffusers have a distinct advantage in creating smaller micro-droplets than Ultrasonic and Nebulizing Diffusers. The micro-droplets produced by Fan Diffusers are about 10 micrometers in diameter. These essential oil micro-droplets undergo a rapid size reduction as the molecules readily evaporate in the air. The micro-droplets are rarely visible for more than one second, yet the essential oil aroma is rather strong.

A couple of rules apply to the evaporation of essential oil molecules from the woven filter cartridges. First, small molecules (Monoterpenes) evaporate quicker than larger molecules (Sesquiterpenes). Second, the looser the weave of the fibers, the quicker the evaporation rate of essential oil molecules. Third, when the filter cartridge weave is tight, it will hold more drops of essential oil and provide longer diffusion time.

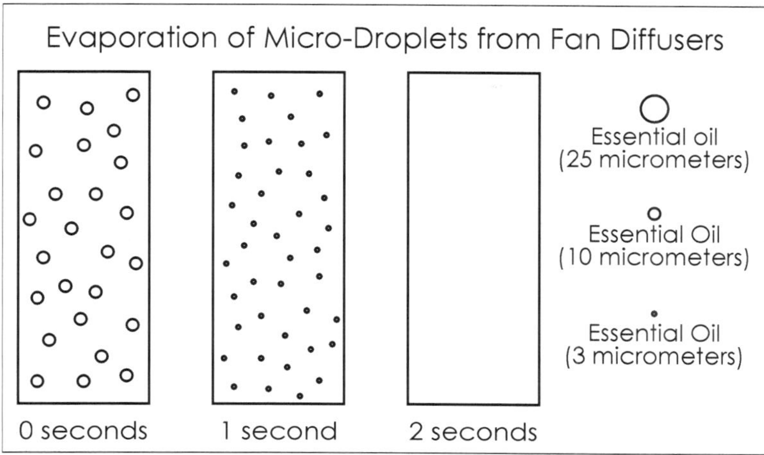

Figure 55. Time-lapse depiction of essential oil micro-droplets produced by Fan Diffusers.

The mist produced by Fan Diffusers appears more transparent and less visible than the mist produced by Nebulizing Diffusers. That is because the micro-droplet size is very small. Fan Diffusers can produce enough airborne aroma to satisfy most users.

Special Features of Fan Diffusers. Fan Diffusers are typically operated at low voltages. Sometimes they are operated by 12-volt DC car battery and by 5-volt DC USB power. Some Fan Diffusers can be operated using 1.5-volt DC rechargeable batteries, allowing them to be taken on trips, in cars, on picnics, and to offices.

What People <u>Like</u> about Fan Diffusers. One of the greatest features of Fan Diffusers is the ease and quickness in exchanging filter cartridges. People also like the very low noise level of the high speed mini-fan. They also like the nearly invisible micro-droplets of pure essential oil. Best of all they like the very low maintenance required to keep Fan Diffusers running.

People like Fan Diffusers because the filter cartridges can be used almost indefinitely, even when discolored by cold-pressed citrus oils. People like the flexibility of using tight-weave or loose-weave filter cartridges. They also like the flexibility of mixing essential oils on the filter cartridge.

People also like Fan Diffusers for their compact size and portable nature. Fan Diffusers can be your car diffuser, your travel diffuser, or your office diffuser. People like the low price tag and the long lifespan of Fan Diffusers.

What People Dislike about Fan Diffusers. Some people dislike Fan Diffusers because they do not appear to match the volume of essential oil vapors that are emitted from the Nebulizing and Ultrasonic Diffusers. Some people complain that Fan Diffusers have a short operational time per essential oil application. Some people do not like re-applying essential oil to the filter cartridge every 3 hours.

Distilled Essential Oils with Fan Diffusers. Steam distilled and hydro-distilled essential oils are great choices for Fan Diffusers. They do a great job of evaporating and diffusing Monoterpene-rich essential oils. They do a decent job evaporating Sesquiterpene-rich essential oils. Fan Diffusers are suitable for diffusing thick essential oils (e.g., vetiver and myrrh) over many hours or days.

Cold-Pressed Citrus Essential Oils with Fan Diffusers. Cold-pressed citrus oils are good candidates for Fan Diffusers. After the smaller molecules have evaporated, they leave behind a colorful stain on the filter cartridge. The harmless color stain comes from large Tetraterpene molecules.

HEAT DIFFUSERS

Heat Diffusers are usually shunned by most essential oil purists. There is always a possibility that the high heat can cause chemical changes in essential oil molecules. The simplest Heat Diffuser uses a burning candle or light bulb to provide heat to evaporate essential oil molecules. New electronic Heat Diffusers use resistive coil heating powered by 12-volt DC car batteries, 110-volt

AC house outlets, or 5-volt DC power using USB connectors to evaporate essential oil molecules.

Operating Instructions for Heat Diffusers. For plug-in resistive coil Heat Diffusers, simply fill the shallow reservoir with a few drops of essential oil. Plug in the Heat Diffuser. The heat from the resistance coil evaporates the essential oil molecules. The rising heat waves push the essential oil micro-droplets into the air above the diffuser.

For candle flame and light bulb Heat Diffusers, simply fill the plastic, metal or ceramic reservoir plate with essential oil, adjust the height of the unlit candle under the reservoir, and light the candle. The candle flame or light bulb will heat up the plastic, metal or ceramic reservoir to energize the essential oil molecules.

Technical Description. Plug-in resistive coil Heat Diffusers are powered by 110-volt AC power located in your home, by 12-volt DC car connectors, or by 5-volt DC USB connectors. The electrical coil embedded in the device will immediately warm up. The heat will energize the molecules in the essential oil to increase their evaporation rate.

Evaporation of Micro-Droplets from Heat Diffusers. Heat Diffusers are not very popular with essential oil purists because of the risk of chemical transformation of essential oil molecules. However, the micro-droplet diameter produced by Heat Diffusers is smaller than the micro-droplets produced by Fan Diffusers. The mist produced by Heat Diffusers is almost invisible. Within less than 1 second, the micro-droplets are too small to see. The mist can sometimes be detected by the diffraction of light.

Special Features. Heat Diffusers have few moving parts. The resistive coil Heat Diffusers are portable and convenient. They are commonly used in cars and computers via their USB connection. The candle Heat Diffusers are portable and decorative. They can be moved into different rooms within the house. The candle acts as a decoration when entertaining guests and provides a calming feeling during cold winter months.

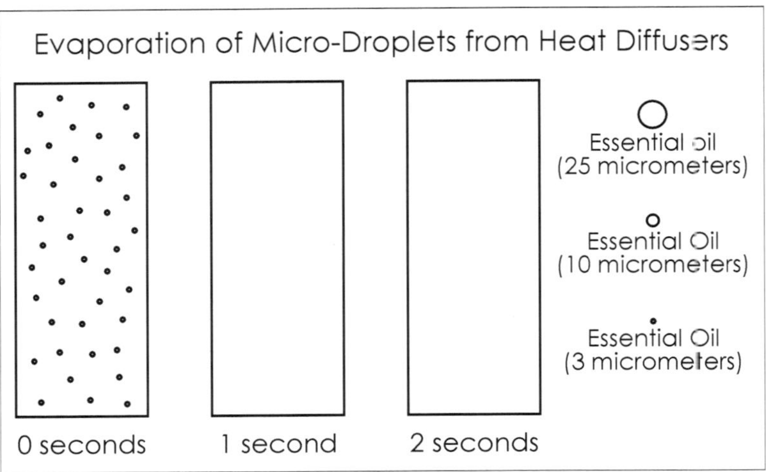

Figure 56. Time-lapse depiction of essential oil micro-droplets produced by Heat Diffusers.

What People <u>Like</u> about Heat Diffusers. People like Heat Diffusers because they are very affordable. They also like Heat Diffusers because they produce zero noise. Yes, they are completely quiet. People also like them because they utilize pure essential oils and produce nearly invisible essential oil micro-droplets.

What People <u>Dislike</u> about Heat Diffusers. Some people dislike Heat Diffusers because of the risk of fire and spilling flammable essential oil. A number of people complain that resistive coil Heat Diffusers do not last more than a week or month. Others dislike Heat Diffusers because they produce gummy residue. Finally, some people dislike Heat Diffusers due to the possibility of chemical changes to essential oil molecules.

Distilled Essential Oils with Heat Diffusers. Heat Diffusers provide a great answer for diffusing steam distilled and hydro-distilled essential oils. Heat Diffusers do a better job at evaporating small-sized molecules (Monoterpenes and Oxygenated Monoterpenes) than larger-sized molecules (Sesquiterpenes, Oxygenated Sesquiterpenes, and Diterpenes).

Heat helps evaporate molecules quicker than with room temperature diffusion with Ultrasonic Diffusers, Nebulizing Diffusers, and Fan Diffusers. Heat increases the evaporation rate of all molecules. The molecules in steam distilled and hydro-distilled essential oils are almost completely evaporated with Heat Diffusers. Heat Diffusers may leave behind a small residue of molecules when diffusing thick essential oils like myrrh.

Cold-pressed Citrus Essential Oils with Heat Diffusers. Cold-pressed citrus oils leave behind a sticky residue of Tetraterpene, Coumarin, and Furanocoumarin molecules in Heat Diffusers. If the build-up of this sticky residue is not cleaned with isopropyl alcohol (rubbing alcohol), then it will lead to the overheating and failure of resistive coil Heat Diffusers.

The Four Active Diffusers. Each of these Active Diffusers has unique features and benefits. Each diffuser produces essential oil micro-droplets of differing sizes. Use these helpful hints and diagrams to help you choose the best diffuser for the right location in your house, car, and office. Choose the right essential oils for your diffusers. Keep your diffusers operational by cleaning off sticky residues and hard water deposits.

EXPLORING SUMMARY

- There are four classes of electrical/mechanical Active Diffusers: Ultrasonic, Nebulizing, Fan, and Heat.
- The four Active Diffusers produce different sizes of essential oil micro-droplets.
- The essential oil molecules quickly evaporate in the rising air from micro-droplets.
- Ultrasonic diffusion will <u>sometimes</u> leave a <u>slight</u> residue of heavy Sesquiterpene, Oxygenated Sesquiterpene, and Diterpene molecules from <u>steam distilled and hydro-distilled</u> essential oils.

- Ultrasonic diffusion will always leave a sticky residue of heavy Coumarin, Furanocoumarin, and Tetraterpene molecules from cold-pressed citrus oils.
- Hard water deposits are common for Ultrasonic Diffusers.
- Heat Diffusers increase the evaporation rate of essential oil molecules.

GLOSSARY

Active diffuser: An electrical, mechanical, or heated device producing a rising mist of essential oil micro-droplets in the air. They are used to fill rooms with the aroma of essential oils. There are four types of Active Diffusers: Ultrasonic, Nebulizing, Fan, and Heat.

Micro-droplet: A very, small spherical droplet of water or essential oil produced by Active Diffusers.

Soft water: Describing household water that contains low levels of dissolved calcium and magnesium minerals. It is typically sourced from municipal surface water and household treated water.

Micrometer: A measure equivalent to 1 millionth of a meter. There are 25,400 micrometers in an inch. The average person can see individual micro-droplets as small as 30-40 micrometer. Micro-droplets as small as 3 micrometer are invisible to the eyes.

Hard water: Describing household water that contains high levels of dissolved calcium and magnesium minerals typically sourced from municipal ground water.

Ultrasonic diffuser: An electrical device that uses a high-frequency piezo oscillator to create vibrations through a reservoir of water and essential oil in order to produce a rising mist of essential oil and water micro-droplets.

Nebulizing diffuser: An electrical device that uses evaporative siphoning of essential oil and high-speed airflow to create a rising mist of essential oil micro-droplets.

Fan diffuser: An electrical device that uses high speed air from an electric fan to evaporate essential oil molecules absorbed on a woven filter cartridge.

Heat diffuser: An electrical device that uses resistive coil heat or light bulb heat to energize essential oil molecules to evaporate into the air. A device using a burning candle to warm up essential oil molecules to increase their evaporation.

DR. WOOLLEY'S CHALLENGE

- Explain to a child or adult the difference between Active Diffusers and Passive Diffusers.
- List the four types of Active Diffusers and categorize the ones you have in your house.
- List three unique features or benefits of Ultrasonic, Nebulizing, Fan, and Heat Diffusers.
- Draw or copy the mist micro-droplets produced by Ultrasonic and Nebulizing Diffusers.
- Organize and list the 4 Active Diffusers in order of least-to-most maintenance.
- Organize and list the 4 Active Diffusers in order of longest, undisturbed diffusing time.
-

15

Diffusing Essential Oils with Passive Diffusers

Unlike Active Diffusers that push essential oil molecules into the air with the aid of electricity, wind, or heat; **Passive Diffusers** simply allow essential oil molecules to escape into the air without assistance. Passive Diffusers do not use electrical or mechanical energy to "push" essential oil molecules into the air.

There are two categories of Passive Diffusers: one that is worn on the body like jewelry: **Portable Diffusers**, and another that is a fixture, furnishing, or decoration within the house, office, or car: **Stationary Diffusers**. The aroma released from these Passive Diffusers depends on the diffuser material and the ambient air temperature.

EVAPORATION OF MOLECULES FROM PASSIVE DIFFUSERS

When a drop of essential oil is placed on a Passive Diffuser, the molecules escape into the air based on their **evaporation rate**. Monoterpene and Oxygenated Monoterpene molecules readily evaporate from the surface of Passive Diffusers. Sesquiterpene,

Oxygenated Sesquiterpene, and Diterpene molecules have lower evaporation rates so they slowly escape from the surface of Passive Diffusers. Tetraterpene molecules found in cold-pressed citrus oils are so large they do not evaporate from the surface of Passive Diffusers. Therefore, they leave a colored stain on Passive Diffusers.

The temperature of the Passive Diffuser greatly affects the **speed of evaporation** of essential oil molecules. The higher the temperature of the Passive Diffuser, the greater the evaporation rate of essential oil molecules. At a typical indoor room temperature of 72°F (22°C), Sesquiterpene molecules slowly evaporate over a period of 1-6 hours. However, at the typical skin temperature of 98°F (34°C), these same molecules are more energized to escape into the air within 1-3 hours.

You can demonstrate this temperature effect by placing a drop of frankincense essential oil on an unglazed ceramic necklace. If you place the ceramic necklace on the countertop, the smaller Monoterpene and Oxygenated Monoterpene molecules readily evaporate; giving off a "piney and lemony" aroma. At room temperature, the frankincense Monoterpene and Oxygenated Monoterpene molecules will last about 60 minutes. Conversely, the larger Sesquiterpene molecules in frankincense will last for about 6-8 hours on the ceramic necklace.

Conversely, when you place the ceramic jewelry around the neck, your surface body temperature energizes the essential oil molecules to 98°F (34°C). Your body heat increases the evaporation rate of all essential oil molecules. At your surface body temperature, the frankincense Monoterpene and Oxygenated Monoterpene molecules will only last 10-15 minutes; and Sesquiterpene molecules will dissipate in about 1-3 hours. Your surface body temperature increases the evaporation rate of molecules approximately 5-fold over room temperature.

Portable Diffusers

You carry and wear Portable Diffusers wherever you work, play, eat, travel, and sleep. They are the jewelry you wear, they are in your pockets, or they are in your purse or wallet. Portable

Diffusers are widely used for the benefit of diffusing essential oils close to your body. I've organized Portable Diffusers into six groups: skin diffusers, jewelry diffusers, pocket/purse diffusers, fabric diffusers, paper diffusers, and toy diffusers.

Skin Diffuser. This one is a bit obvious. When you place a drop of essential oil on your skin, YOU become a Portable Diffuser. A portion of the essential oil molecules penetrates into your skin and a portion evaporates from your skin. Your skin is composed of an outer layer called the **epidermis** (over the skin), a layer below that is called the **dermis** (skin), and a third layer called the **hypodermis** (beneath the skin).

The epidermis (12 micrometers thick for hairy skin and 16 micrometers thick for hairless skin) contains a thin, outer layer of flat, dry cells covering a thicker, inner layer of plump, vibrant skin cells. The epidermis is about as thick as a sheet of paper.

The dermis is composed of nerve fibers, blood vessels, sweat glands, hair follicles, and hair roots. For hairless skin, the dermis is only 50 skin cells thick (1500 micrometers), while for hairy skin, the dermis is twice a thick–100 skin cells thick (3000 micrometers).

The hypodermis (sometimes referred to as subcutaneous layer or subcutis) is composed of fatty tissue, collagen, and larger blood vessels. The hypodermis is about 2000 micrometers thick. Fatty tissues act like a hotel for essential oil molecules to reside for days, weeks, and months.

The essential oil molecules that penetrate into your skin will either enter your blood stream, deposit in fatty tissue, or slowly migrate out of your skin into the air. Monoterpene and Oxygenated Monoterpene molecules easily penetrate the epidermis, dermis and hypodermis layers. These molecules readily enter the blood stream. They also enter the fatty tissues of the hypodermis. Fatty tissues retain essential oil molecules like a sponge holds water. Fatty tissues slowly release Monoterpene and Oxygenated Monoterpene molecules over hours, days, and weeks.

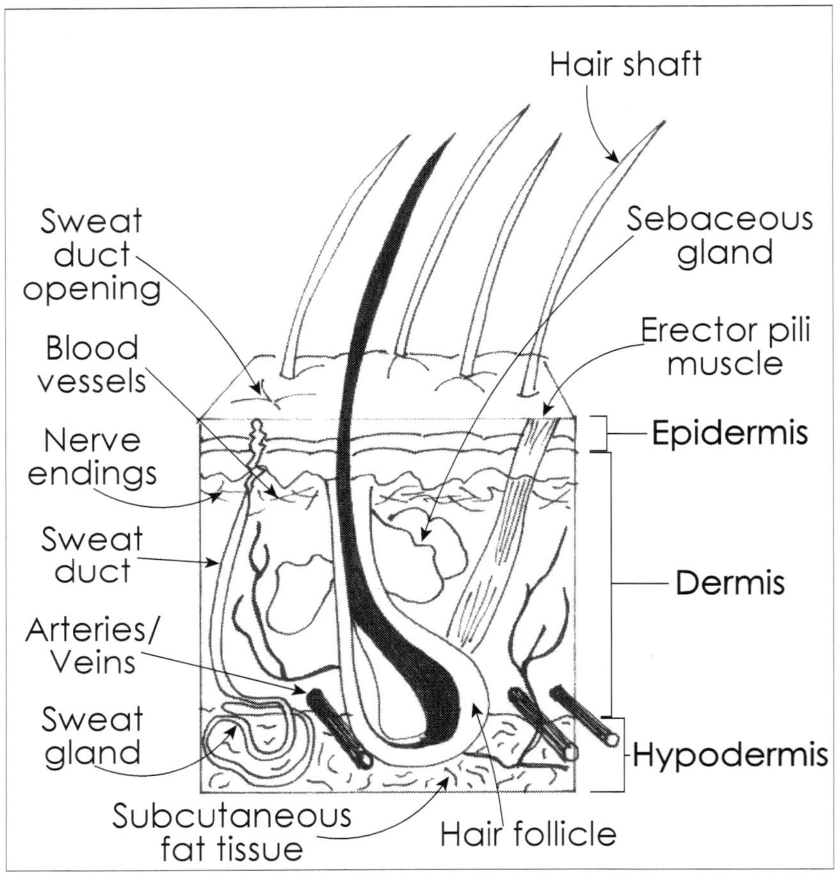

Figure 57. Schematic drawing of the epidermis, dermis, and hypodermis of hairy skin.

Sesquiterpene, Oxygenated Sesquiterpene and Diterpene molecules do not easily penetrate the epidermis. These larger molecules require carrier molecules like Monoterpenes and Oxygenated Monoterpenes to assist them through the dry epidermal layer. These carrier molecules are called **skin penetration enhancers**. They help open up micro-channels in the epidermis and carry the larger Sesquiterpene and Diterpene molecules through the epidermis, dermis, and hypodermis. It is as if Monoterpenes are giving Sesquiterpenes a piggy-back ride. These larger molecules can be carried into the bloodstream with the help of skin penetration enhancer molecules. When they enter fatty tissues, they tend to stay for weeks and months.

Think of your skin as a great way to get essential oil molecules into your bloodstream and provides a warm surface to energize and diffuse essential oil molecules into the air around you. Your skin has a high surface area and many places where you can apply essential oils. When you want to use your skin as a passive diffuser, place a drop of essential oil on a hairy portion of skin.

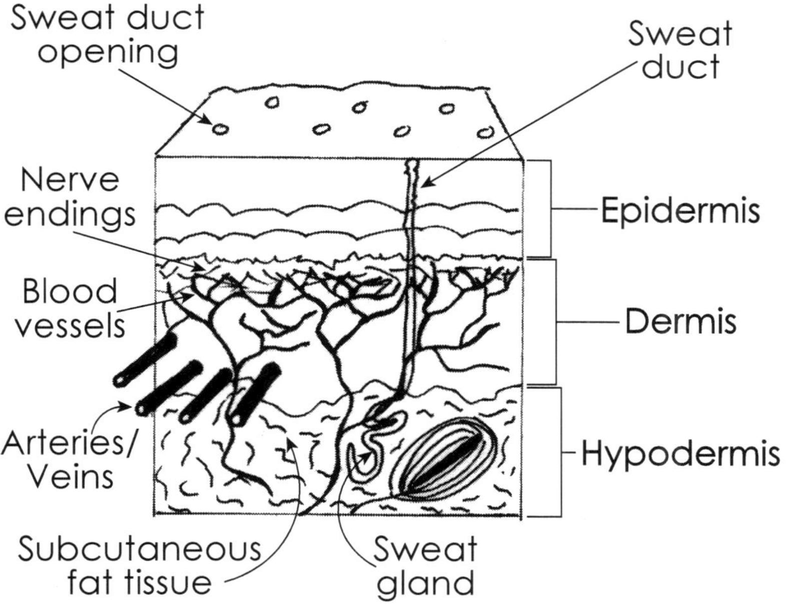

Figure 58. Schematic drawing of the epidermis, dermis, and hypodermis of hairless skin.

When you want to increase the uptake of essential oil molecules into your bloodstream, place a drop on a hairless portion of skin. Hairless skin is thin and has more blood vessels reaching the vibrant skin cells close to the epidermis. In addition, when you apply essential oils after a shower, bath, sauna, or workout, you will notice an increase in the molecules that enter your skin and bloodstream.

Recall that Coumarins and Furanocoumarins in cold-pressed citrus oils can create a photosensitive reaction (inflammation and long-lasting dark burn) when applied to the skin prior to sun exposure. The levels of Coumarins and Furanocoumarins in cold-pressed lime, bergamot, grapefruit and lemon essential oils are relatively high. When applying these oils to the skin prior to sun exposure, you can dilute them with carrier oils, lotion, creams or other essential oils to reduce the risk of skin photosensitivity.

Jewelry Diffusers. Jewelry Diffusers may be any ornament that you wear on your wrists, ankles, neck, ears, head, or waist. They may be a decorative accessory in your hair or pinned to your shirt, pants, dress, or blouse. Jewelry Diffusers may be made of finely designed metal with a felt pad to apply the essential oil. Other jewelry diffusers are made of beautifully designed ceramic, beautiful wooden beads, carved leather, or finely woven string.

Metallic jewelry diffusers

1. Elegant stainless steel and silver look
2. High price
3. Moderate-to-high essential oil loading capacity
4. Exchangeable felt pads for different oils
5. Excellent body heat conductor to evaporate molecules
6. Ceramic jewelry diffusers
7. Semi-elegant, relaxed look
8. Moderate price
9. High essential oil loading capacity
10. Mixing of previously used oils
11. Moderate body heat conductor to evaporate molecules

Wooden jewelry diffusers

1. Casual, organic look
2. Low-to-moderate price
3. High essential oil loading capacity
4. Mixing of previously used oils
5. Low-to-moderate body heat conductor to evaporate molecules

Leather/String jewelry diffusers

1. Casual, organic look
2. Low-to-moderate price
3. Moderate-to-high essential oil loading capacity
4. Mixing of previously used oils
5. Low-to-moderate body heat conductor to evaporate molecules

Pocket/purse diffusers. Some of the best and least expensive Passive Diffusers are pocket and purse diffusers. Pocket diffusers can be any material that will absorb drops of essential oil, like leather, fabric, paper, ceramic, wood, or plastic.

Purse diffusers can be the purse or wallet itself (especially the inside of leather purses or wallets) or any of its contents. They may be items in your purse (leather wallet, paper money, key chain, handkerchief, ceramic "coin", etc.). My personal favorite pocket diffusers are a clean handkerchief and my wallet. My hand touches one of these almost every hour. I love inhaling essential oils that are meant for me.

Leather diffusers

1. Leather wallet (inside and out), leather wallet strap, leather coin purse, leather belt
2. Leather purse (inside and out), leather purse strap, leather money clip, leather wristband

Fabric diffusers

1. Fabric scarf, fabric head band, fabric handkerchief
2. Fabric hair ribbon, fabric hair piece

Metallic/Ceramic diffusers

1. Metal jewelry diffuser, ceramic jewelry diffuser
2. Ceramic coin, ceramic key chain

Wooden/Plastic diffusers

1. Hair brush, hair comb, hair piece, watchband

Fabric diffusers. Some clothing accessories double as Passive Diffusers. They may be items that you wear from time-to-time or a clothing accessory that you frequently wear (scarf, hat, hair ribbon, hair band, hair comb, leather belt, leather shoes, etc.). No one wants to stain their clothes with essential oils. Fortunately, most steam distilled and hydro-distilled oils will not leave a stain. Since cold-pressed citrus oils contain Tetraterpene pigments that typically leave colored stains, I place drops of citrus oil where the colored stain will not show. Here are a few suggestions based on my experience.

I like wearing baseball caps, so I have learned to place a couple of drops of peppermint, lavender, juniper, Taiwan red hinoki, orange, grapefruit or tangerine on the underside of the bill. I have even tried placing oils on the inside trim of the cap. With these locations, any Tetraterpene stains from the cold-pressed citrus essential oils will not be visible.

Leather clothing makes great Passive Diffusers. I have often used my leather belts and leather shoes as Passive Diffusers when I'm doing business. I prefer Sesquiterpene-rich essential oils on leather because it stays around for days and weeks. I consider my leather wallet, leather briefcase, and leather-bound planner as part of my clothing. I'm always using my wallet or its contents as Passive Diffusers.

In the winter, I often wear earmuffs to stay warm. A drop of essential oil on each side can help me stay alert. One of my favorite clothing diffusers is my handkerchief. A couple of drops of cedarwood, Taiwan red hinoki, or juniper will last for days. Instead of blowing my nose into my handkerchief, I inhale essential oil aromas to keep me alert, focused, and engaged.

Paper diffusers. Paper diffusers are a great way to store and release essential oil molecules. You can scent your business cards with your favorite essential oil. Place your scented business cards in your jacket, blouse, or shirt. Place a few drops of orange, frankincense, or geranium essential oil on the edges of business cards before your business meetings.

Consider using your planner, journal, or reading material as paper diffusers. I prefer using the inside covers of personal books to retain essential oils. Sometimes I place a line of essential oil on the paper edge of books. When I open these personal books, I want to be relaxed and focused. I want my mind to be centered on planning or meditating.

You can add essential oils to your paper money prior to making a purchase. When you store paper money diffusers in your leather wallet, the leather traps the essential oil molecules. Paper business cards and paper money stored in your wallet or purse can be a great source of low-cost, replaceable diffusers of essential oil molecules. My favorite paper diffusers are paper money and business cards.

Toy diffusers. Toy diffusers are a special class of Portable Diffusers. Those cute, cuddly, stuffed animals and baby blankets that little children take to bed for naps or for nighttime sleep are perfect Passive Diffusers. Your child's favorite stuffed toy is usually cuddled close to the face. Add a couple of drops of "relaxing" essential oil for naps and bedtime.

Your toddler's favorite blanket can be a great Passive Diffuser. Lavender essential oil applied to a baby blanket can calm and relax a child. Both the toy and the natural aroma send a signal to the child's brain saying, "comfort", "security", "relax", and "sleep". Your older children and teenagers may want to keep their comfort blanket at bedtime for its relaxing aroma. Even adults have a favorite blanket, comforter, slippers, or house gown that can act as Passive Diffusers.

Therapeutic fidget devices are a great opportunity to convert into Portable Diffusers. These cubes, spinners, etc. are often recommended for children who fidget in organized classroom settings. Adults often fidget with hand-held devices that can act as Portable Diffusers; including pens, pencils, erasers, wooden balls, dice, and many others to stay focused on tasks. Adding a drop of essential oil can enhance these fidget devices into "focus" devices.

One of the benefits of Portable Diffusers is to keep the essential oils close to you. Some of the most expensive essential oils are placed on Portable Diffusers in order to keep the aroma cloud close to the body and continuously working for you.

Stationary Diffusers

Stationary Diffusers are usually a permanent fixture, an adjustable furnishing, or a room decoration in your house, office, or car. Stationary Diffusers passively emit essential oil molecules into the environment. They are natural air fresheners for living space. These fixed-location diffusers are intended to freshen the air for all who enter. Stationary Diffusers can be made from almost any material, including wood, ceramic, wax, metal, glass, plastic, leather, fabric, paper, etc.

Stationary Diffusers are best known for their therapeutic benefits. Adding a drop of peppermint oil to a library furnishing can encourage "alertness" to the mind and body. A drop of lavender essential oil to a bathroom throw rug can help "relax" the mind and body after a long day of work. Adding a drop of geranium essential oil on a kitchen decoration can create a room that is "beautiful" to the mind and body. Stationary Diffusers are therapeutic devices.

Another common need for Stationary Diffusers is to mask foul-smelling odors in bathrooms and kitchens. Other common uses for Stationary Diffusers occur with unexpected passing-gas episodes, mildew aromas in basements, lingering cigarette smoke aromas, changing diapers, toddler mishaps, sour milk in carpets, pet odors, and many others. A drop or two of essential oil placed on Stationary Diffusers are great at disguising and eliminating foul odors. Essential oils are a natural solution to foul household odors. Essential oils can help guests feel comfortable visiting your house.

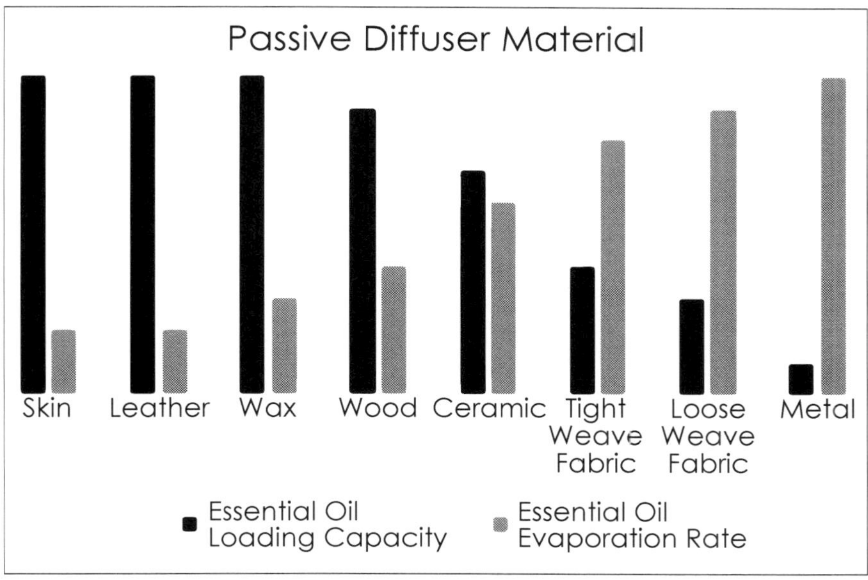

Figure 59. Diagram of the relative essential oil loading capacities and essential oil evaporation rates for Passive Diffuser compositions.

Essential Oils for Stationary Diffusers

You need to learn to choose the right essential oil for the therapeutic or aroma effect you desire. Some essential oils can quickly fill the room with therapeutic aroma. Some oils can change foul odors into pleasant ones. Some essential oils are great at lingering for days and days.

Monoterpene-Rich Essential Oils for Stationary Diffusers. Monoterpene molecules evaporate quickly and fill the room within 5 minutes. The aroma strength dissipates as the molecules spread throughout the house. Monoterpene-rich essential oils are a welcoming signal to guests who visit your bathrooms. These are some Monoterpene-rich essential oils I like to use: orange, lemon, lime, tangerine, grapefruit, frankincense, hinoki, pine, and fir.

Oxygenated Monoterpene-Rich Essential Oils for Stationary Diffusers. These essential oils provide flowery and floral aromas to create a pleasant environment. Oxygenated Monoterpene-rich essential oils linger longer than Monoterpene molecules. They work well creating therapeutic and pleasing conditions in your living room, TV room, kitchen, dining room and bedrooms. Here are a few Oxygenated Monoterpene-rich oils that I have used: lavender geranium, lemongrass, cinnamon bark, eucalyptus, ylang ylang, and peppermint.

Sesquiterpene-Rich Essential Oils for Stationary Diffusers. Sesquiterpene-rich essential oils create aroma-filled rooms that say "confidence and strength". Sesquiterpene-rich oils have a lasting "woody" aroma. Sesquiterpene molecules evaporate slowly so they linger in rooms for days and weeks. Sesquiterpene molecules do not fill the room quickly, but you will be blessed with the long-lasting, subtle aroma. Here are some Sesquiterpene-rich essential oils I like to use: cedarwood, juniper, Taiwan red hinoki, and sandalwood.

Stationary Diffusers for Bathrooms

Bathrooms are a persistent source of foul odors. The foul odors come from unflushed toilets, waste build-up around toilets, bathroom garbage cans, soap scum on the bath or shower, and rings of grime in the sink. They also originate from a putrid stench of eliminations, soiled diapers, and toddler mishaps.

Keep a couple of bottles of essential oils in plain view in the bathroom. That way, family members and guests feel at-ease using essential oils to help hide and dissipate any foul odors. Just add one or two drops of essential oils to any bathroom Stationary Diffuser to keep your bathroom smelling fresh. You may want to use a spray bottle with water and essential oil to spray the bathroom after each use. All of these Stationary Diffusers work. Just add a drop of essential oil on them and make a happy, confident exit.

Bathroom Fixtures: toilet bowl, toilet seat, bathtub, shower stall, bathroom sink

Bathroom Furnishings: bath mat in tub, toilet seat cover, shower mat, garbage can, bathroom rugs, roll of toilet paper

Bathroom Decorations: bowl of beach sand, bowl of seashells, wooden sculpture, unscented/unlit wax candle, wooden sticks in a vase, decorative ceramic tile

Stationary Diffusers for Kitchens

The foul odors in the kitchen may depend on your kitchen design, ventilation, housecleaning habits, the types of food you cook, the method of cooking, and how food waste is disposed. Some of the foulest aromas come from the garbage can, the garbage disposal, the cutting board, and the refrigerator.

Overripe or outdated foods can produce unpleasant aromas. Onions, strong-smelling fruits and vegetables, and meat scraps chopped on a cutting board can generate lingering odors. The kitchen is one room in the house that needs to have a pleasant, inviting aroma.

Kitchen Fixtures: Kitchen sink, garbage disposal, ceramic floor tiles, refrigerator, countertops, dishwasher, trash compactor, cabinets

Kitchen Furnishings: kitchen garbage can, kitchen throw rug, paper towel holder, paper towel roll, dry dish cloth, broom bristles, lid on canned food, dish scrubber, bar soap, kitchen apron, and apron pocket diffusers

Kitchen Decorations: floral decoration (artificial, wooden or dry flowers), wooden balls, beach sand/shells in a bowl, wooden sculpture, wooden bowl, unscented/unlit wide candle, folded cloth serviette, folded paper towel, refrigerator magnets

Stationary Diffusers for Bedrooms

The bedroom is a place of relaxation, recovery, and rejuvenation. Sleeping helps the body and mind refresh themselves for another day. Lavender essential oil assists with relaxation, meditation, restfulness, and sleep. Using Stationary Diffusers in the bedrooms can help trigger the desired emotional/body state, the proper state of action, and the preferred state of mind.

Bedroom fixtures: bed frame, inside dresser drawers, carpet, closet, desk drawers, chair

Bedroom furnishings: garbage can, closet hangers, pillows, dirty clothes hamper

Bedroom decorations: sachet, wax candles, wooden sculpture, string of beads, flower arrangements, wall hangings, award statue, posters

Stationary Diffusers for Basements and Laundry Rooms

Basements tend to be cool and damp. This dampness can foster mildew and spore-producing molds on walls, ceilings, carpeting, and carpeting pad. Spore-producing molds emit a molecule called geosmin. Geosmin creates an aroma typically described as "muddy" or "damp soil". Hiding this constant "damp" aroma can be accomplished with Active Diffusers and Stationary Diffusers.

Laundry rooms tend to have lingering odors. Dirty clothing or wet laundry can create "damp-musty" aromas at times. Sometimes it can be a challenge to keep the laundry room smelling fresh and inviting. Fortunately, essential oils applied to Stationary Diffusers can keep laundry rooms clean and refreshing.

Basement & Laundry fixtures: carpeting, laundry sink, large floor rug, floor tile, vinyl flooring, cabinets, washer, dryer

Basement & Laundry furnishings: throw rugs, garbage cans, couch, couch cushion, floor pillows, mop, broom, dust mop, ironing board, drying rack, vacuum cleaner

Basement & Laundry decorations: unscented/unlit candles, decorative shelves, wall hangings, posters

Stationary Diffusers for Recreation Rooms

Recreation and exercise rooms are wonderful places to relieve stress and get fit. If cardiovascular exercise or weight training is being performed, then the room may take on the aroma of perspiration.

Your child's playroom may become the place of spilled milk or ground-in cookies. The area surrounding your pool table or ping pong table may be a constant place for snacks, drinks, and meals. Rancid smells, stinky exercise equipment, and spilled drinks can generate unpleasant odors. Using essential oils on Stationary Diffusers can quickly improve the aroma of your recreation rooms.

Recreation fixtures: carpeting, floor tiles, wood flooring, exercise equipment, ceiling fan blades

Recreation furnishings: throw rugs, garbage cans, floor pillow, toys, cabinets, stuffed animals

Recreation decorations: wax candles, decorative shelves, wall hangings

Stationary Diffusers for Entertainment Rooms

Rooms for reading books and viewing the television are places for meditation and relaxation. Diffusing essential oils can create the desired mood for family rooms, TV rooms, and the library. Unfortunately, these entertainment rooms are often places for eating snacks and meals. Dropped crumbs, spilled drinks, and splotches of grease can lead to foul odors. Essential oils placed on Stationary Diffusers can help overshadow unwanted odors and invite family members and guests to enjoy a pleasing, relaxing environment.

Entertainment fixtures: carpeting, floor rugs, vinyl flooring, wood flooring

Entertainment furnishings: throw rugs, couch, couch cushions, fireplace, garbage cans, chairs, tables, ventilation filters

Entertainment decorations: wooden sculptures, edge of unwanted books, DVD case with inserted paper towel

Stationary Diffusers for Home Office and Business Offices

The mood and feeling of offices at home or at work can be created using essential oils. Essential oils can create the proper mood for business meetings. For example, orange or geranium essential oils can keep people alert, focused, and awake. In addition, lavender and frankincense essential oils can create an office setting for focused study, recreational reading, or relaxing meditation.

Office fixtures: carpeting, floor rugs, vinyl flooring, wood flooring, cubicle dividers

Office furnishings: throw rugs, desk, desk drawers, chairs, pen holder, pen cap, business card holder, business cards

Office decorations: wooden sculptures, unscented/unlit candles, wall hangings, silk plants

Stationary Diffusers for Cars

How much coffee, hot chocolate, soda drinks, and juice boxes have been spilled on carpets and upholstery in the average car? How many crumbs have been embedded in the carpeting? How much unseen mold and mildew has grown in moist carpeting and carpet padding? The soles of shoes can deposit the foulest smelling stains on carpets, floor rugs, and floor mats in your car. Hurrah for the wonderful aroma of totally natural essential oils on Stationary Diffusers in your cars!

Car fixtures: carpeting, glove box, cup holder, steering wheel, seats

Car furnishings: floor mats, child car seats, floor rugs

Car decorations: hanging cardboard decoration, hanging stuffed animal, hanging wooden beads, hanging woven decoration, hanging bottle diffuser, steering wheel cover

SUMMARY

I love passive Stationary Diffusers. Most of my essential oil diffusing utilizes Stationary Diffusers inside my house and my car. Be creative. Consider your needs and use your oils. I am also a fan of passive Mobile Diffusers. I often use my leather wallet, paper money, paper business cards, and the lower brim of my baseball caps as Portable Diffusers for essential oils.

EXPLORING SUMMARY

- There are two classes of Passive Diffusers: Portable Diffusers and Stationary Diffusers.
- Portable Diffusers are carried around with you as you accomplish your daily tasks.
- Stationary Diffusers are fixtures, furnishings, and decorations in your house, car, and office.
- The evaporation rates of essential oil molecules are highly dependent on temperature.
- Monoterpene-rich and Oxygenated Monoterpene-rich essential oils applied to Passive Diffusers produce an instant aroma cloud.
- Sesquiterpene-rich essential oils provide a long-lasting aroma.

GLOSSARY

Passive Diffuser: An object that absorbs essential oil then allows the molecules to evaporate at room temperature or surface body temperature. There are two types of Passive diffusers: Portable and Stationary.

Portable Diffuser: A Passive Diffuser that can be worn on the body to release a cloud of essential oil molecules wherever the body goes. There are six classes of Portable Diffusers: skin diffusers, jewelry diffusers, pocket/purse diffusers, fabric diffusers, paper diffusers, and toy diffusers.

Stationary Diffuser: A Passive Diffuser that has a fixed location in the house, office, or car to release a cloud of essential oil molecules into the surrounding environment. There are three classes of Stationary Diffusers: fixture diffusers, furnishing diffusers, and decoration diffusers.

Evaporation Rate: Describing the number of molecules or percent of molecules that escape the liquid phase (essential oil) to go into the gas phase (air).

Speed of Evaporation: Describing the time it takes for essential oil molecules to escape the liquid phase (essential oil) to go into the gas phase (air).

Epidermis: The outer layer of skin, meaning "over the skin". It is composed of a thin outer layer of flat, dry skin cells covering an inner layer of plump, vibrant skin cells.

Dermis: The middle layer of skin, meaning "skin". It is composed of nerve fibers, blood vessels, sweat glands, hair follicles, and hair roots.

Hypodermis: The inner layer of skin, meaning "beneath the skin". It is composed of fatty tissue, collagen, and larger blood vessels.

Skin Penetration Enhancer: Monoterpene molecules that readily penetrate all three layers of skin that can "carry" larger molecules during their journey. These molecules help larger molecules penetrate the skin and get into the bloodstream.

DR. WOOLLEY'S CHALLENGE

- Take 20 minutes to write down as many useful Stationary Diffusers you can find in your house and car.
- Use essential oils on a Mobile Diffuser that you already have in your possession. Record your feelings and the responses from others.
- Try using essential oils on two Stationary Diffusers in your car or house. Did your family notice?
- Take an inventory of your household odors. Start by going outside for 10 minutes, then quickly walk into a room. Take deep breaths and record any foul room odors. Return outside and continue checking the odors of other rooms.

16

How Aromas Change after Applying Essential Oils

One of the main reasons you use essential oils is the **aroma**. You sense the aroma of essential oil molecules using the olfactory nerve receptors in your nasal cavity. One of the wonderful features of essential oils is that once applied to the skin or other surface, the aroma slowly changes. Yes, the **aroma changes** because essential oil molecules evaporate (enter the air) at different rates.

> "I put on lavender essential oil but the smell went away. Where did it go?"
>
> "Why does the smell of sandalwood oil remain on my skin all day?"
>
> "Why does the aroma of frankincense change after being applied to the skin?

This chapter will help you answer these curious questions about how the aroma of an essential oil changes when applied to the skin. Now that you are familiar with the groups of essential oil molecules, you are more prepared to explore aroma changes over time.

AROMA CHANGES = EVAPORATION OF MOLECULES

First, let us review some concepts about essential oil molecules and their properties. Monoterpene molecules have a tendency to be the first molecules to **evaporate** from the skin. Monoterpenes are the smallest molecules that make up essential oils, so they have the highest evaporation rate. Their high evaporation rate means the Monoterpene molecules rapidly escape into the air to provide a strong aroma. Some examples of Monoterpene-rich essential oils are pine, fir, spruce, orange, lemon, tangerine, and frankincense.

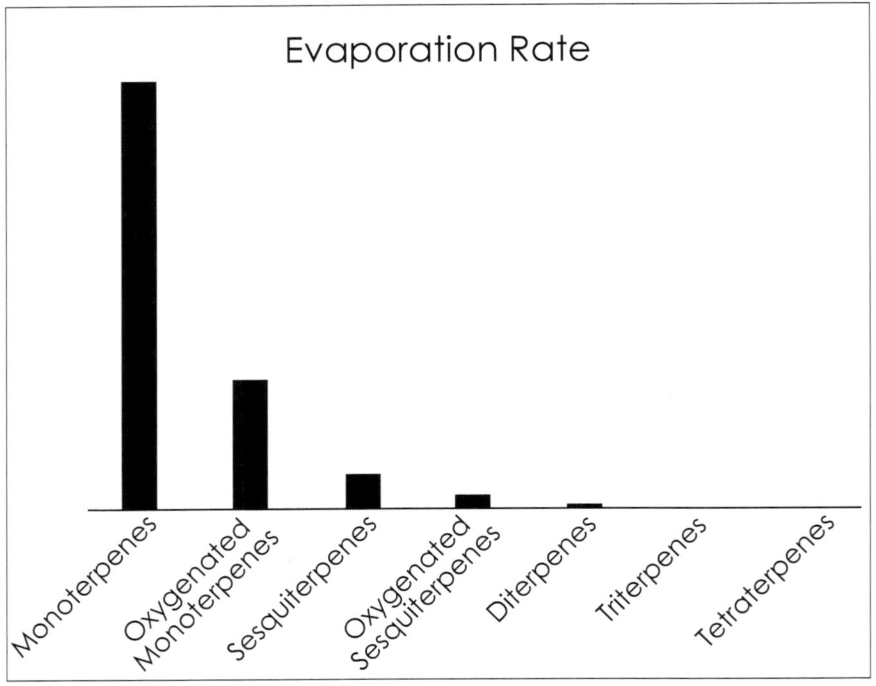

Figure 60. Diagram depicting the relative evaporation rates of essential oil molecules.

Oxygenated Monoterpenes are slightly larger molecules because they contain at least one Oxygen atom. The Oxygen atom creates a stronger interaction between molecules within the liquid essential oil. The Oxygen atom also creates a strong interaction between Oxygenated Monoterpene molecules and water molecules on moist surfaces. Oxygenated Monoterpenes have a slightly lower evaporation rate than Monoterpenes. Some examples of Oxygenated Monoterpene-rich essential oils are lavender, cinnamon bark, clove, and geranium.

Sesquiterpene molecules are one and a half times larger than Monoterpene molecules. Sesquiterpene molecules have a lower tendency to escape from the liquid essential oil into the air. Sesquiterpenes have significantly lower evaporation rates than Monoterpenes. Some Sesquiterpene-rich essential oils include cedarwood and juniper.

Oxygenated Sesquiterpenes have at least one or more Oxygen atoms attached to Sesquiterpene molecules. The addition of Oxygen atoms increases the interaction between these molecules to retain them in the liquid essential oil and on moist surfaces. Oxygenated Sesquiterpenes have a very low evaporation rate so they tend to stay wherever they are applied. Some Oxygenated Sesquiterpene-rich essential oils are Taiwan red hinoki (hong kuai), myrrh, and sandalwood.

Diterpene, Triterpene, and Tetraterpene molecules are even larger than Sesquiterpenes. Diterpene and Triterpene molecules evaporation rates are very, very low. Tetraterpenes have the lowest evaporation rate of all the terpene molecules; it may take them years, decades or centuries to evaporate. The only examples of Tetraterpene-containing essential oils are cold-pressed lime, lemon, grapefruit, mandarin, orange, and tangerine.

EVAPORATION OF MONOTERPENE-RICH ESSENTIAL OIL

Monoterpene essential oil molecules have high evaporation rates, while heavier Sesquiterpene and Diterpene molecules have significantly lower evaporation rates. Molecules with high evaporation rates tend to rapidly and abundantly escape the **liquid phase** to occupy the air in high concentrations. When most of the molecules with high evaporation rates escape into the **gas phase** (air), they leave behind the heavier molecules of lower evaporation rates in the liquid phase. Therefore, the liquid phase tends to become concentrated with large, heavy molecules.

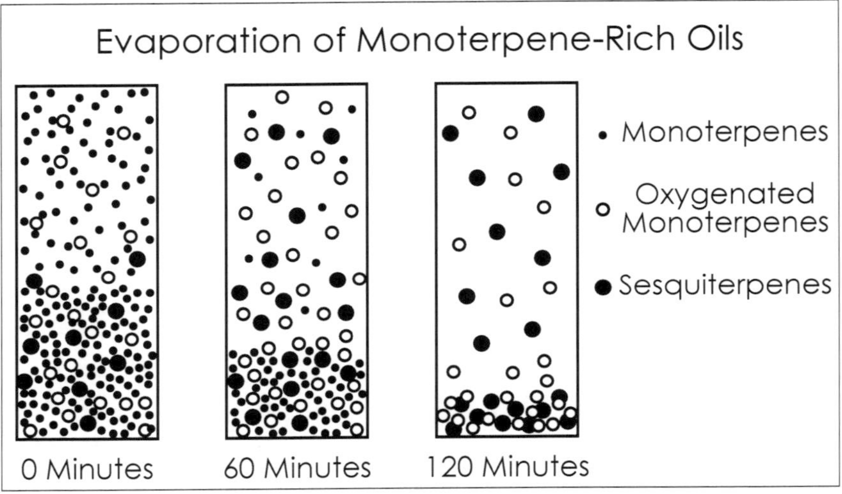

Figure 61. Time-lapse depiction for the evaporation of molecules from Monoterpene-rich essential oils.

Molecules with low evaporation rates are slow to leave the liquid phase, which is why they are difficult to detect with your nose. The molecules with low evaporation rates remain for long hours or days on the skin. During this long duration, the heavy molecules give off only a faint aroma because there are few molecules that leave the liquid phase. Essential oils rich in molecules with low evaporation rates (Sesquiterpene and Diterpene molecules) usually possess a "woody, earthy, spicy" aroma.

Essential oils that are rich in Monoterpene molecules undergo dramatic aroma changes once they are placed on the skin or other surfaces. Here are some common examples of Monoterpene-rich essential oils (more than 50% Monoterpene molecules):

- **Monoterpene-rich Citrus Oils:** orange, lemon, lime, tangerine, grapefruit, mandarin, yuzu, and bergamot.
- **Monoterpene-rich Wood Oils:** balsam fir, black spruce, pine, fir, cypress, tea tree, and hinoki.
- **Monoterpene-rich Oleogum-resin Oils:** elemi, galbanum, sacra frankincense, carterii frankincense, frereana frankincense, and serrata frankincense.
- **Monoterpene-rich Spice Oils:** nutmeg, tarragon, thyme, marjoram, caraway, cumin, dill, and celery seed.
- **Monoterpene-rich Perennial Oils:** goldenrod, cistus, angelica, hyssop, spearmint, eucalyptus, and marjoram.

Aroma changes for Monoterpene-rich carterii frankincense essential oil after applied to the skin:

- 0 minutes: "strong piney, slightly lemony, earthy, frankincense"
- 15 minutes: "piney, slightly lemony, earthy, frankincense"
- 30 minutes: "piney, more lemony, earthy, frankincense"
- 45 minutes: "slightly piney, lemony, slightly earthy, frankincense"
- 60 minutes: "slightly piney, lemony, frankincense, slightly woody"
- 90 minutes: "slightly lemony, frankincense, slightly woody"
- 120 minutes: "slightly lemony, strong frankincense, woody"

These are dramatic aroma changes for carterii frankincense essential oil. In the beginning, the essential oil contains about 80% Monoterpene molecules that provide the "strong piney" aroma right out of the bottle. However, the high evaporation rate of *alpha*-pinene molecules (about 30% in the essential oil) quickly evaporates from the applied oil. The "lemony" aroma comes from the limonene molecules that have one of the lowest evaporation rates of the Monoterpenes.

After 45-60 minutes, the "piney and lemony" aroma finally dissipates as the Monoterpene molecules evaporate from the applied surface. This is when the Oxygenated Monoterpenes begin taking over as the dominant aroma combination and the "woody" aroma from Sesquiterpene molecules becomes more apparent.

After 120 minutes nearly all the Monoterpene and Oxygenated Monoterpene molecules have evaporated from the applied surface. A new long-lasting aroma simply referred to as "frankincense" now remains on the applied surface. The "frankincense woody" aroma remains as an assembly of 20 or more Sesquiterpene molecules and two unique Diterpene molecules, incensol and incensyl acetate.

EVAPORATION OF OXYGENATED MONOTERPENE-RICH ESSENTIAL OIL

The "flowery, sweet, floral" aromas of Oxygenated Monoterpene-rich essential oils undergo minor changes after application to the skin. The main aroma change is usually a drop in aroma-intensity over time as the applied molecules evaporate. Once the Oxygenated Monoterpene molecules evaporate, the applied surface takes on a unique aroma of persistent Sesquiterpene molecules. Essential oils rich in Oxygenated Monoterpenes (more than 50%) include:

- **Monoterpene Alcohols:** lemongrass, geranium, lavender, tea tree, cypress.
- **Monoterpene Aldehydes:** cinnamon bark, lemongrass, melissa, eucalyptus.
- **Monoterpene Ketones:** peppermint, spearmint, caraway, white camphor, helichrysum.
- **Monoterpene Esters:** Roman chamomile, lavender, geranium, cinnamon bark.
- **Monoterpene Oxide:** *Eucalyptus globulus*, *Eucalyptus radiata*, rosemary, myrtle.

Aroma changes for Oxygenated Monoterpene-rich lavender essential oil after applied to the skin:

- 0 minutes: "floral, strong lavender, slightly sweet, strong herbal, spicy"
- 15 minutes: "slightly floral, strong lavender, slightly sweet, herbal, slightly spicy"
- 30 minutes: "strong lavender, slightly sweet, herbal, faint woody"
- 45 minutes: "lavender, herbal, sweet ester, faint woody"
- 60 minutes: "lavender, sweet ester, faint woody"
- 90 minutes: "slightly lavender, sweet ester, faint woody"
- 120 minutes: "sweet ester, woody"

The aroma changes over time for lavender essential oil are like reading a good adventure or mystery novel; always a new discovery with every chapter. Each 15-minute aroma chapter of lavender brings out a new aroma composition. This is an aroma change that you will have to try yourself.

After 60 minutes the aroma of the applied lavender oil begins to be less of a broad bouquet as the Monoterpene molecules evaporate. From 60 – 120 minutes the aroma changes as the major Oxygenated Monoterpene molecules linalool, linalyl acetate and lavandulyl acetate evaporate from the skin.

After 120 minutes the aroma of the applied lavender has more of a singular aroma. Some of the Monoterpene esters remain to produce a "sweet ester" aroma. In addition, the Sesquiterpene molecules provide a "slight woody" aroma.

EVAPORATION OF SESQUITERPENE-RICH ESSENTIAL OILS

This section will include Sesquiterpene and Oxygenated Sesquiterpene molecules. These molecules have low evaporation rates, so they remain on the skin for a long time.

Since these molecules have such low evaporation rates, you may need to move your nose close to the skin to detect them. Very few of these larger molecules escape the liquid phase, which makes them hard to detect. The Sesquiterpene molecules tend to have an aroma of "woody, earthy, spicy". Here are several examples of essential oils that are rich in Sesquiterpene molecules:

- **Sesquiterpene-rich Wood:** cedarwood, blue cypress, Taiwan red hinoki
- **Sesquiterpene-rich Oleogum-resin:** myrrh, elemi, copaiba
- **Sesquiterpene-rich Spice:** ginger, black pepper, vitex
- **Sesquiterpene-rich Root:** valerian, ginger, vetiver
- **Sesquiterpene-rich Flower:** ylang ylang, German chamomile, yarrow, patchouli, goldenrod, melissa

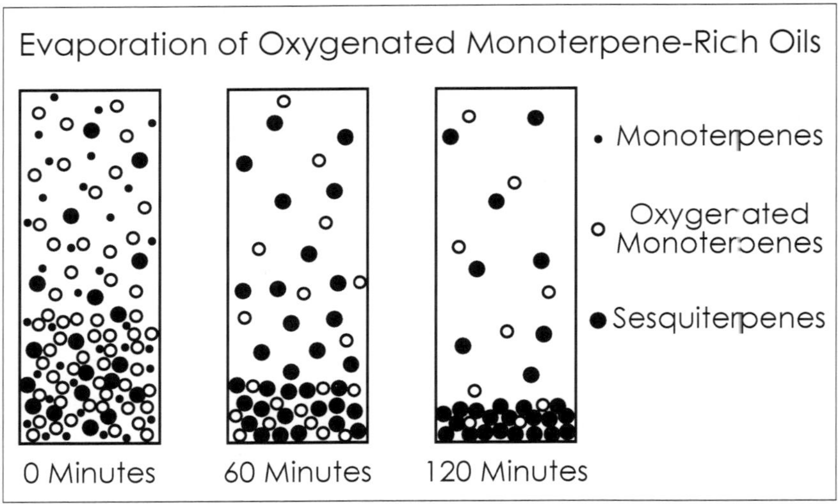

Figure 62. Time-lapse depiction for the evaporation of molecules from Oxygenated Monoterpene-rich essential oils.

The aroma of cedarwood essential oil remains the same for hours due to the great abundance (more than 95%) of Sesquiterpene molecules. The aroma of valerian root essential oil remains nearly constant over days due to its high abundance of Oxygenated Sesquiterpene molecules. Myrrh essential oil contains about 90% Sesquiterpene molecules and most of the remainder as Oxygenated Sesquiterpene molecules. So it is no surprise that there is little change in the aroma of myrrh essential oil over time.

Oxygenated Sesquiterpenes have a similar "woody, spicy" aroma as Sesquiterpenes (except for the unique Sesquiterpene Aldehydes that emit a "citrus, orange" aroma). Here are several examples of essential oils that are rich in Oxygenated Sesquiterpene or contain unique Oxygenated Sesquiterpene molecules:

Oxygenated Sesquiterpene Alcohols: Taiwan red hinoki (hong kuai), sandalwood, blue cypress, myrrh, patchouli (with the general aroma described as "woody, floral, spicy, sweet").

Oxygenated Sesquiterpene Ketones: ginger, grapefruit, vetiver, cedarwood (with the general aroma as "woody, spicy, warm").

Oxygenated Sesquiterpene Aldehydes: orange, bergamot, mandarin, tangerine, clementine, blood orange (with the general aroma described as "citrus, orange, sweet").

Aroma changes for Sesquiterpene-rich cedarwood essential oil after applied to the skin:

- 0 minutes: "woody, earthy, leathery, sweet, slightly fruity, slightly musky, slightly spicy"
- 15 minutes: "woody, earthy, leathery, sweet, slightly fruity, slightly musky"
- 30 minutes: "woody, earthy, leathery, slightly sweet"
- 45 minutes: "woody, earthy, leathery, slightly sweet"
- 60 minutes: "woody, earthy, leathery"
- 90 minutes: "woody, earthy, leathery"
- 120 minutes: "woody, earthy, leathery"

The aroma changes for Sesquiterpene-rich and Oxygenated Sesquiterpene-rich essential oils are not very noticeable. The aroma usually starts out "woody" and stays "woody" for hours, days, and weeks. The aroma of cedarwood essential oil is no different.

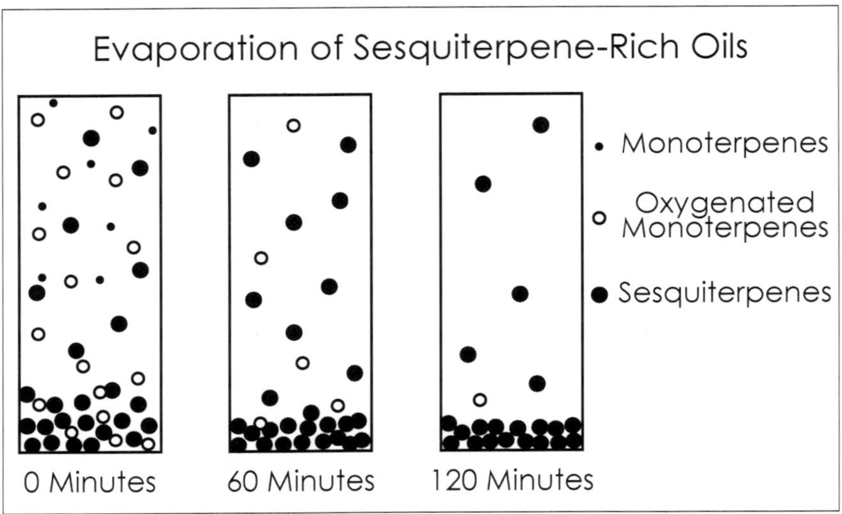

Figure 63. Time-lapse depiction for the evaporation of molecules from Sesquiterpene-rich essential oils.

Cedarwood essential oil contains less than 0.5% Monoterpenes, less than 0.5% Oxygenated Monoterpenes, about 90% Sesquiterpene molecules and about 10% Oxygenated Sesquiterpene molecules. There are three Sesquiterpene molecules that dominate the aroma: *beta*-himachalene (45%), *alpha*-himachalene (15%), and *gamma*-himachalene (10%). Cedarwood essential oil has a unique, long-lasting aroma.

The aroma of cedarwood essential oil starts out complex as "woody, earthy, leathery, sweet, slightly fruity, slightly musky, slightly spicy." A small 6-Carbon molecule, mesityl oxide, may be responsible for the initial, fleeting "musty pungent" aroma. The brief "sweet, fruity" aroma likely comes from a 9-Carbon molecule, *para*-methylacetylphenone. These two unique essential oil molecules evaporate in less than 60 minutes. After the first hour the aroma of cedarwood essential oil remains constant for hours and days.

EVAPORATION OF DITERPENE, TRITERPENE & TETRATERPENE MOLECULES

Diterpene and Oxygenated Diterpene molecules have a slightly noticeable aroma. These molecules will stay on the skin until washed off with soap.

Triterpene and Tetraterpene molecules have very, very low evaporation rates at room temperatures and surface body temperatures. These molecules tend to remain on applied surfaces as sticky or waxy residues. Triterpene and Tetraterpene molecules exhibit almost no aroma. These Triterpene and Tetraterpene molecules stay on the skin and other surfaces. Here are some examples of Tetraterpene-containing essential oils:

Tetraterpenes and Oxygenated Tetraterpenes: lime, bergamot, lemon, grapefruit, tangerine, mandarin, clementine, orange

Aroma changes for Tetraterpene-containing lemon essential oil after applied to the skin:

- 0 minutes: "sweet, lemony, citrus, tropical, fruity, slightly piney"
- 15 minutes: "lemony, citrus, fruity, tropical, slightly sweet, slightly piney, slightly earthy"
- 30 minutes: "lemony, citrus, fruity, tropical, slightly earthy"
- 45 minutes: "lemony, citrus, slightly fruity, slightly tropical"
- 60 minutes: "lemony, slightly citrus, faintly tropical"
- 90 minutes: "slightly lemony, slightly citrus"
- 120 minutes: "faintly lemony, faintly citrus"

The aroma starts out intense because lemon oil is dominated by Monoterpene molecules (over 90%). The aroma of lemon essential oil is dominated by limonene (about 65%) in the first 60 minutes. The slightly "piney" aroma comes from, among others, *alpha*-pinene and *gamma*-terpinene molecules. There are unique aldehyde molecules (less than 1%) in lemon oil (octanal, nonanal, decanal, and undecanal) that provide an initial "fruity" aroma. The "tropical" aroma of lemon oil comes from *cis-beta-*ocimene and *trans-beta-*ocimene molecules.

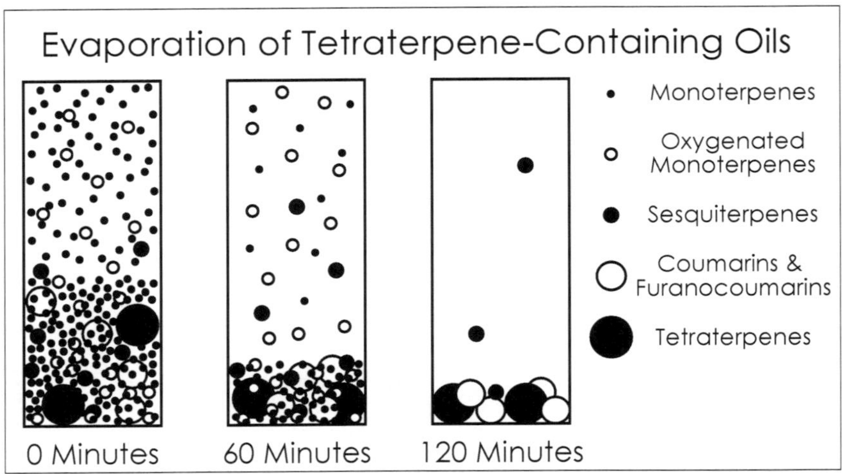

Figure 64. Time-lapse depiction for the evaporation of molecules from Tetraterpene-containing cold-pressed citrus essential oils.

After 60 minutes the intensities of the aromas greatly diminish. The volume of lemon essential oil on the skin is less than half of the original. Most of the Monoterpene molecules have evaporated. There is still a dominant aroma of "lemon" because the limonene molecule is so abundant in the original lemon oil.

After 120 minutes, most of the aroma of lemon oil is not easily detected. There is still a slight aroma of "lemon" from residual limonene molecules. In addition, the large Coumarin and Furanocoumarin molecules provide some "citrus" quality. Finally, Tetraterpene and Oxygenated Tetraterpene molecules in lemon oil leave a slight color stain. These molecules are so large they do not give off much of an aroma. These large molecules are usually scrubbed off the skin with soap long before they would have a chance to evaporate.

AROMA CHANGES

Knowing the chemistry and aroma of the groups of terpene molecules can help you describe the aroma changes of essential oils. That same knowledge can assist you in describing the aroma changes as the essential oil molecules evaporate from your skin. Knowing how aroma changes occurs should help you create your own essential oil blends. I hope you feel a sense of confidence at you help people understand the aroma changes that occur with essential oils.

EXPLORING SUMMARY

- Aroma changes occur with most essential oils after applied to the skin or other surfaces.
- Monoterpene-rich essential oils show dramatic aroma changes in the first 30 minutes as the highly volatile molecules escape from the skin or other surfaces.
- Oxygenated Monoterpene-rich essential oils undergo constant aroma changes over the first 2 hours after application. The aroma of these essential oils typically lasts 1-2 hours.
- Sesquiterpene-rich and Oxygenated Sesquiterpene-rich essential oils contain mainly molecules with low evaporation rates. The aroma undergoes only slight changes over time. The aroma can last for days.

GLOSSARY

Aroma: The complex description of odor molecules detected by olfactory nerve endings and decoded by the brain.

Aroma Change: The detected aroma of molecules from essential oils applied to the skin or other surface as a function of time.

Evaporation: The process when molecules are energized enough to escape the liquid phase on the skin and enter the gas phase (air).

Liquid phase: Where essential oil molecules are contained within a liquid or liquid film.

Gas phase: Where essential oil molecules are randomly free to move about in the air.

DR. WOOLLEY'S CHALLENGE

- Draw or copy the diagrams showing how the molecules in Monoterpene-rich essential oils evaporate. Show the molecules at 0 minutes, 60 minutes and 120 minutes.
- Draw or copy the diagrams showing how the molecules in Oxygenated Monoterpene-rich essential oils evaporate. Show the molecules at 0 minutes, 60 minutes and 120 minutes.
- Draw or copy the diagrams showing how the molecules in Sesquiterpene-rich essential oils evaporate. Show the molecules at 0 minutes, 60 minutes and 120 minutes.
- Describe to a child or adult the aroma change (over a 2 hour period) of carterii frankincense essential oil placed on the skin.

17

How to Share Your Experiences

You were ready to share essential oil experiences with other people before you started reading this book. Now you have added knowledge and understanding to confidently share your experiences. I designed the Dr. Woolley's Challenges to help you share your newfound knowledge after each chapter.

Remember that the purpose of this book is to help you to feel confident. You have learned some new technical words and new concepts regarding essential oils. You can now see and describe more of the invisible world of essential oil molecules. You are ready to share your essential oil experiences with better understanding.

SHARE THE EXPERIENCES

You may have shared your first essential oil experience within days of opening your initial bottle. At the time, you did not need to know all the chemistry vocabulary. In addition, you did not need to persuade people that your essential oils were the best. At the time, you did not need to explain how essential oils affect the human body.

When you took your first sniff of an opened bottle of orange essential oil, you felt "alive", "invigorated", or "refreshed". You may have started DAY 1 by sharing this experience with your friends and relatives via social media. It is normal to share experiences involving new products. That is why essential oils are so easy to share.

When you applied lavender essential oil to your feet for the first time, you likely felt "relaxed", "calm", or "sleepy". You may have shared that experience with a friend or loved one. You may have shared it with your friends on social media. Maybe you emailed a friend to explain how lavender essential oil makes you feel.

When you first massaged peppermint essential oil on your temples after a tense day, you probably felt "cool", "refreshed", or "relieved". That is a wonderful experience to share! Many people are looking for a product that will help them relax after a tense day at work.

At the time, you simply shared your first essential oil experiences in your own words. That was perfect! However, now that you have acquired an expanded vocabulary regarding essential oils you are prepared to paint your essential oil experiences with vibrant colors.

SHARE THE SIMPLE

I have tried to keep this book simple. Yes, I know there are many new words and concepts. The Dr. Woolley's Challenges were designed for you to gain confidence in describing essential oils, essential oil molecules, and essential oil aromas. Your expanded vocabulary should give you that confidence. Hopefully, you now see essential oils with a greater understanding and appreciation. Now you can enhance your essential oil sharing-experiences with some simple technical phrases.

Now, when you share your lavender essential oil experiences you can add some simple phrases from this book. "Lavender essential oil molecules are released from harvested lavender flowers and leaves by Steam Distillation." You can also add, "I like lavender essential oil because of the flowery aroma."

Now, when you share your experiences with peppermint essential oil, you can add flair with other simple phrases. "Peppermint essential oil looks like a drop of water, but it is more complex. It is composed of about 200 different molecules. Each molecule has its own aroma. Each molecule provides its own health benefits. I like peppermint essential oil because it comes from Nature."

SHARE THE ORIGINS

Most of your friends and relatives have no idea where essential oils come from. You need to let them know that they are naturally produced by plants in forests and farms. Share with them how plants produce and store essential oils. Share with them how essential oils are used by plants.

Now, when you share your experiences with lavender essential oil, you can add a phrase or two about the origins of lavender. "Lavender essential oil is produced by lavender plants. Most of the lavender essential oil is stored in small hairs that cover the surface of lavender leaves and lavender flowers. The essential oil helps protect the lavender plants from being eaten by insects and animals. Lavender plants also use their essential oil to communicate; 'Do not eat me, but sit down next to me and relax.' To humans, lavender essential oil communicates; 'Slow down, take a rest, you can feel calm now.' That is why I love lavender essential oil."

SHARE THE CHEMISTRY

You may want to expand your personal essential oil experiences by adding some phrases about chemistry. This may be helpful when you talk to a university student, scientist, dentist, nurse, or medical doctor. They may open their minds when technical terms are used to describe your essential oil experiences. They live in a technical world.

Now, when you share your personal experiences of peppermint essential oil, you may want to share a bit of chemistry. "This peppermint essential oil has been tested by GC-MS to ensure it has the correct molecules and composition. Peppermint essential oil is mainly composed of menthol. Menthol causes a cooling sensation when applied to the skin. This peppermint essential oil can be ingested because it is on the Generally Regarded As Safe (GRAS) list by the FDA. I take a drop of peppermint essential oil on my tongue when my stomach is upset."

Now, when you share your frankincense essential oil experience, you can provide some insights on how it is distilled. "This frankincense essential oil is hydro-distilled from the oleogum-resin that is collected from the frankincense tree. The species is known as *Boswellia carterii*. It is sometimes called carterii frankincense. The frankincense oleogum-resin is collected by the native tribes of northern Somalia. They are the only ones who inherited the rights to collect frankincense oleogum-resin. I like the aroma of frankincense essential oil because it helps me concentrate and focus."

Now, when you share your personal experiences with lemon essential oil, you can add some helpful hints about its natural origin. "My lemon essential oil is cold-pressed from the peels of lemon fruits. The lemon essential oil is released from the peel using tiny stainless steel spikes on conveyer rollers that transport the lemon fruits. The lemon oil is sprayed off the fruit peel with water. The lemon oil and water are separated because the lemon essential oil floats on the water. After the lemon oil is expressed, the fruits are cut in half and juiced. The cold-pressing of lemon essential oil takes place in the same facility where lemon juice is produced. Every time I smell my lemon oil it is like taking my body and mind to an exotic paradise."

SHARE THE USES

The chapters on diffusing essential oils gave you hundreds of ways to use essential oils in houses, offices, and cars. I described four Active Diffusers and many different Passive Diffusers that will help you enjoy essential oils in your daily life.

Now, you can share with your friends ten ways to use orange essential oil in your house. "I love my orange essential oil. I use it in my ultrasonic diffuser in the kitchen each morning. The aroma helps my kids get ready to school. I know it helps them wake up. The aroma of orange also helps keep my kitchen smelling fresh and clean. I also use orange essential oil in the bathroom to disguise foul odors. I put a drop of orange oil in the garbage can or on my throw rug. I use orange oil in my nebulizing diffuser before guests arrive for dinner. I even diffuse orange oil when my kids come home from school to do their homework because it helps them concentrate."

SHARE THE CONFIDENCE

The more you understand and experience, the more you can share. Find new ways to use essential oils. Use new phrases to describe the origins, chemistry, and uses of essential oils. Every day you will become more confident as you share essential oils.

Share with your friends how this book helped you. Let them know that you memorized phrases from this book. Show them the diagrams and photos in this book. Invite them to invest in their own copy. Encourage them to gain the same confidence you have achieved.

About the Author

Cole L. Woolley, PhD, is an expert at simplifying technical concepts of essential oils and teaching their uses, properties, and potentials to the general public. He enjoys using essential oils and promoting their benefits towards health, happiness, and emotional well-being. Dr. Woolley began analyzing essential oils while completing his doctoral degree at Brigham Young University. Dr. Woolley is an analytical chemist with world-wide expertise in analyzing essential oils using gas chromatography, GC-MS, and chiral GC-MS. He has traveled the world as a scientist, an inventor, a businessman, a writer, a product developer, a marketer, and a speaker. In his spare time he enjoys activities with his family, researching family history, trail running in the mountains of Utah, gardening, botany, sports, travel, cultures, classical art, and classical music.

Facebook: Cole Woolley, PhD – Exploring Essential Oils
www.ExploringEO.com

Made in the USA
San Bernardino, CA
13 September 2017